J ack held out an arm, and Lacey took it, glad for his warmth on the cool beach. They ambled along behind the kids, just at the edge of the surf. Here only a gentle rolling wave teased their feet once in a while. After the first one, Lacey began to enjoy it.

"Now, admit that it wouldn't be nearly as much fun to be walking up there on the dry sand with your shoes on," Jack said. His arm slipped around her naturally, and he matched her pace easily. Lacey liked the way their bodies fit together, especially here in this moonlit place between land and sea.

"You're right," she murmured over the breakers. "If you look out toward the ocean you can pretend you're out in the middle of nowhere instead of on a little strip of public beach. It's very relaxing."

They turned around to follow the kids toward the parking lot. The children ran, laughing and talking with each other, up the packed sand near the waves. Jack and Lacey strolled along, still at the water's edge, getting farther and farther behind. In a moment Jack stopped.

"You've got the nicest hands," he said, looking down at the one he held in his. "I know that sounds ridiculous, but I keep noticing that. The first time I picked you up off the rink floor I noticed them. They're so beautifully shaped." He brought her hand up to his mouth and nuzzled the palm, taking away any rejoinder Lacey was about to make.

She stood there, mesmerized....

A PALISADES CONTEMPORARY ROMANCE

Dalton's DILEMMA

LYNN BULOCK

PALISADES

DALTON'S DILEMMA
published by Palisades
a division of Multnomah Publishers, Inc.
and in association with the literary agency of Writer's House, Inc.

©1998 by Lynn Bulock
International Standard Book Number: 1-57673-238-X

Cover illustration by Paul Bachem
Design by Brenda McGee

Scripture quotations are from:
The Holy Bible, New International Version (NIV)
©1973, 1984 by International Bible Society,
used by permission of Zondervan Publishing House
The Holy Bible, King James Version (KJV)

Palisades is a trademark of Multnomah Publishers, Inc.,
and is registered in the U.S. Patent and Trademark Office.

Printed in the United States of America

For information:
MULTNOMAH PUBLISHERS, INC.
POST OFFICE BOX 1720
SISTERS, OREGON 97759

Library of Congress Cataloging-in-Publication Data
Bulock, Lynn.
    Dalton's dilemma / by Lynn Bulock.
    p. cm.
    ISBN 1-57673-238-X (alk. paper)
    I. Title.
    PS3552.U463D35 1998
    813'.54—dc21   98–13725
                                            CIP

98 99 00 01 02 03 04 — 10 9 8 7 6 5 4 3 2 1

To Joe, always

*And to my two wonderful friends,
the best support anybody could have—
Lynn M. and Diane—
you two have no idea how much you have to do with my writing!*

Therefore, I urge you, brothers, in view of God's mercy,
to offer your bodies as living sacrifices, holy and pleasing to God—
this is your spiritual act of worship.
Do not conform any longer to the pattern of this world,
but be transformed by the renewing of your mind.
Then you will be able to test and approve what God's will is—
his good, pleasing and perfect will.

ROMANS 12:1–2 (NIV)

One

It was the fast-food clerk's "ma'am" that sent Lacey Robbins over the edge. True, it was just one more little annoyance in a fairly normal, though trying, day, but that "ma'am" as in, "You forgot your change, ma'am," was all it took to fray Lacey's nerves the last little bit.

Her first impulse was to shriek at the teenager behind the counter at Taco Time. "I am only twenty-eight years old. I'm nobody's idea of a ma'am," her beleaguered brain argued.

Logic took over in a moment. She was in a typical fast-food restaurant at noon on Saturday, accompanied by three squabbling children. Why wouldn't the counter clerk call her ma'am? Lacey sighed, thanked the teenager, took her nearly forgotten change, and went to the table where her nieces and nephew were involved in one of their interminable arguments.

This one was worse than usual because it was in public, they had spent the entire Christmas break together, and everybody was cranky because Brooke was gone. Taking her oldest niece to the Orlando airport to go back to college had been harder than Lacey expected.

So now here she was, carrying a heavily laden tray across the tile floor of a place utterly devoid of any charm whatsoever so that she could feed three ungrateful, sniping kids. What a wonderful life.

Orlando always looked strange decorated for Christmas, and this year was no different. Lacey surveyed the tatty silver tinsel hung in garlands across the ceiling. It looked tired. So did the Santa outside. Manger scenes made a little more sense with palm trees around them; somehow Bethlehem had more

9

in common with sunny Orlando than it did with the North Pole.

Still, it was time for all of the commercial trappings of Christmas to come down so they could all get on with life. Lacey was just thankful to get through another holiday season without major upheaval, and was wishing that this day would finish too.

Becca and Brittany were still in the thick of some heated discussion when Lacey put the tray on the table. Brian seemed to be playing both sides, interjecting remarks intended to drive the pitch of both of his sisters' voices even higher.

"Kids, it sounds like cats in a sack over here. Cut it out so we can eat or I'm taking everything to the van, got it?" Lacey said, sounding more snappish than she intended.

"Got it," Brittany sighed, sliding over so Lacey could sit in the booth with them. "Did you get mine plain, with no tomatoes? You know I don't like tomatoes."

Last week tomatoes had been all right, and it had been black olives that were the hated topping. "I got you nachos, with just cheese and beans and sour cream," Lacey said, putting the item down in front of the six-year-old.

"Two tacos and a beef burrito over here," she told Brian, putting his meal down in front of him where he sat across from her with a slight scowl. "And a light chicken taco and a diet soda over here," she said, placing Becca's food at her place.

The tray was emptying out fast. "Crumbs!" Lacey exclaimed. "I forgot to get myself anything but diet soda."

"So go back up and get something," Becca said in a tone that suggested that she believed advancing senility would claim what little remained of her aunt's brain soon. "We can stay here without you. It took long enough anyway."

"You were the one that wanted to come here," Brian argued.

"You said if you saw one more french fry you were going to gag, remember?"

"All too well. And eating lunch sitting next to you makes me want to gag anyway," his sister retorted.

"All right. That's enough!" Lacey said, setting her drink down harder than she intended on the scarred orange surface of the table. A little geyser of sticky brown liquid came out of the hole in the top of the cup, dousing her wrist and silencing the children.

She grabbed a napkin and wiped off the liquid, sorry that she had lost her cool in public with the children. Just because they were having a bad day didn't mean she should too, she told herself. "Let's ask the blessing and eat," she said quietly. Silently they did just that, and when she looked up again, it was to see Brian's hand slipping over onto her side of the table.

"Take one of my tacos, Aunt Lacey. I don't want you to have to go back in line," he said. He looked more like his father every day, chestnut hair in waves around his thin face. She felt bad when he did things like this, using his thin ten-year-old shoulders to hold her problems.

"Thank you, Bri. I do believe I'll take you up on that offer," she said, knowing that refusing would hurt his feelings more than taking the food at this point. He needs a father, a voice whispered in her ear.

As if I didn't know that, Lord, she said silently back. He had a heavenly Father, and that would have to be enough for now because Lacey had no idea how she would ever go about providing the earthly kind. She had been parenting this mob for three years now, since her older sister and her husband died. Lacey had long ago resigned herself to the fact that volunteers for a second date were few and far between when you had four kids.

11

Lacey nibbled her taco and considered what the applicant would have to be like. He'd have to be strong in his faith or she couldn't consider him. And given her circumstances, he needed to be part colossus and part teenager to put up with this crew, a genius at conflict resolution for the War of the Hot Water, and a tactful diplomat to face Becca's attempts at fashion. He'd need the flexibility of a rubber man and the patience of Job. And, Lacey smiled to herself as she finished her drink, being a real looker wouldn't hurt either.

"What's so funny?" Becca asked her. For a change it wasn't a challenge but more of an interested question. Lacey thought to herself that she was going to smile more often if she could get civil talk from her teenager just by doing it.

"Nothing, really. I was just thinking I needed to change my New Year's resolution. I'm in a rut. We're all in a rut. I think it's time I resolved to seek adventure."

"Adventure?" This time Becca's tone said "yeah, right" as she quirked one eyebrow.

"That clerk called me 'ma'am' when I forgot my change," Lacey explained. "I am not old enough to be a ma'am, even if I do have you four. I mean, I'm not all that much older than Brooke."

"Brooke is nineteen. You're twenty-eight. That's nine years older. Almost as long as Brian is old," Brittany said.

"I know. But it doesn't feel that much older," Lacey explained to her while trying to refrain from wincing. "And it's time I remembered that, like Brooke, I still have a lot of life to live."

"I miss her already," Brittany sighed. "How long until she comes back for Easter?"

"Months. She's only been gone a few hours," Lacey said, touching the tip of Britt's nose. "She isn't even back at school in Atlanta by now."

"Can we call her tomorrow?" Brittany looked wistful.

"She'll call us," Lacey said. The ever-organized Brooke wouldn't miss a Sunday phone call home, even if she was still settling into the dorm. Brooke. It was still such a surprise to Lacey that the child had grown up. When had she changed from a pudgy four-year-old in a dance-recital panda suit to the smiling, self-possessed young woman they had left at the airport this morning?

They were so different. Lacey was tall, but Brooke was taller. Where Lacey's honey hair usually fell straight and unruly around her face and onto her shoulders, Brooke was always well put together, heavy French braid smooth. As usual, she had looked so calm and collected today. It had been such a contrast to Lacey's own emotions swirling around inside as she watched Brooke leave.

Now Brooke was halfway to Atlanta, and Lacey's emotions were still churning. There was a dull, empty ache in her most of the time lately, a nameless hole. She had prayed about it, thought about it, but it was still there, and still she could not put a finger on what it was that she was missing.

She wasn't lonely. This mob never gave her time to be lonely. Running a tax accounting business out of their home and running kids to their various activities at school and church, sports and scouts, there was never time to be lonely. And she wasn't bored. No time for that either. But there was definitely something missing.

"So this seeking adventure thing," Brian broke into her thoughts. "How does it work?"

Trust Brian, her dreamer, to want to know that part. "You know, I don't have a clue," Lacey told him. "I just believe that's what I need. What do you want to do this afternoon?"

Three voices chimed in at once, and someone voted down

every suggestion. Movies? Nobody could agree on one that sounded good. The park was boring. Just going home was out of the question. "We're never going to figure it out," Brittany said dramatically, flinging a hand away from her.

The movement knocked over her drink, which was still partially filled with liquid, sending a pale green puddle over the table. Lacey picked up the remains of the stack of napkins on the tray. Sopping up the mess, she looked down to where the napkins had been.

"I don't remember seeing those," she said, picking up the slips of paper that had been revealed by the napkins.

"They were handing them out when you ordered," Brittany piped up. "What do they say?"

"Half-price entry to Skate Way. Good all weekend January 4th and 5th."

"That's it. That's our adventure," Brittany said.

"I don't know…" Lacey began. A chorus of pleading stopped her.

"We'll be good." "It's something different." "It's an adventure, isn't it?" they all argued.

"Okay. Get the table cleaned off and everybody get out to the van with no squabbling and we'll go," Lacey told them, sure she had bought herself a trip home.

For the first time all day everyone listened to her, and in less than a minute she had three quiet kids in the van. It was obviously meant to be. "Okay, so this is my first adventure," she told them. Starting the van, she felt a thrill go up her spine. She really felt as if she was going on an adventure for a change. And Lacey Robbins, staid accountant and surrogate parent to the wild Horton gang, felt distinctly out of her depth.

Two

It was a quick drive to the rink, which looked much the same way the one in her hometown in Illinois had looked two decades before. A long, squat building, with lots of minivans and station wagons disgorging their cargo of kids and teenagers at the door. When she stopped, Becca hopped out first, eager to go.

Lacey was amazed that Becca would deign to be seen in public with the rest of them. Most of the time she didn't go out before dark with the family. "There has to be something to this," Lacey said to herself, watching Becca amble along in front of her.

Lacey remembered enough about roller rinks to know that a purse would be a definite hindrance. She stuffed her billfold into her front jeans pocket, put car keys in another one, and put her half-empty shoulder bag under the van seat, then closed up and followed the kids.

She was still mystified by the speed at which Becca was entering the building. Then she opened the door to the rink, and, standing in the tiled area getting ready to buy tickets for all of them, Lacey's memory flashed a clear picture. Instead of the tears she'd been afraid of shedding earlier, there was laughter bubbling up inside her, and she knew why Becca had come without a fight.

"What are you laughing at?" Brittany asked, head cocked.

Lacey traced a finger down the child's snub nose, skating off at the end and tickling her. "I just remembered why I did so much roller skating when I was your age. The roller rink was where your mom went to meet your dad." Lacey and Beth's parents hadn't approved of their eldest daughter going steady with the same boy all through high school, even if he was probably bound for the ministry, so the young lovers had found all sorts of strategies.

One of their favorites was called "taking Lacey to the roller rink."

"Mom would drop us off at the rink, and Beth would walk in with me," Lacey explained to the grinning kids lacing up their skates. "Then she'd give me fifty cents for snacks, and if I was lucky I could con Kevin out of the same thing, and that was the last I'd see of either of them for two hours."

Becca giggled as she tried to scope out the possibilities nonchalantly. It was easy for Lacey to see that roller rinks hadn't changed. There were still teenage couples skating, standing in corners, and sitting on benches. Gaggles of girls hung out together, chatting and giggling. And there were still teenage boys trying to look cool while standing up on wheels, hoping to be noticed.

Apparently Becca wanted to do some noticing. If her attitude gave Lacey déjà vu, her face made Lacey feel like she was looking into a mirror. There was the same honey hair, tortured into the latest teen style instead of Lacey's plain straight fall. Green eyes, just as nearsighted as hers, a fact hidden by Becca's contact lenses, instead of her own sensible glasses with their tortoiseshell frames. And the same tall, gangly body Lacey could remember having at that age. There was no sense trying to reassure her that in a few years everything would sort itself out.

Becca was never going to believe at fourteen that her colt legs would eventually get more shape to them, that what felt like a long, skinny frame would stretch out to be lithe and comfortable instead. There were still days when Lacey wondered, looking in a mirror, when she'd made the changes herself.

She'd lost her mother young, and her sister, Beth, had raised her. Somewhere in the awkward, painful years of sorting herself out, Beth had managed to coax her from an angry adolescent to a controlled woman, and now she would have to try to do the same for Beth's daughter.

Lacey fished in her pocket and came out with two dollars. She held the money out to Becca. "Want to pretend you don't know us?" Becca smiled back, a surprisingly mature and friendly smile. "Maybe for a little while. I'll check back in later." Then she skated off to make a nonchalant circle of the concrete floor as the music pulsated.

Lacey finished tying her own skates and stood up gingerly. The laces felt oddly snug around her ankles, while the wheels threatened to zip out from under her. She hadn't been on skates in nearly twenty years. Not since Beth graduated from high school and Kevin proposed, which happened in pretty short order. Of course, her parents hit the roof, but Beth was eighteen and Kevin nineteen and there was little anyone could tell them.

Even three years later when they were living in student housing at the university with a baby, a few pieces of broken-down furniture and a huge student loan, no one could have convinced them they weren't blissfully happy, Lacey reflected. She tested her wheels under her. Just like Beth and Kevin had in their foolish young marriage, so far she was staying upright.

She moved her feet gingerly across the carpet and was surprised at the easy way she seemed to glide across the floor. Of course the rink would be slicker, but apparently she wasn't going to make too big a fool out of herself.

Brian couldn't hide the surprise in his eyes at the sight of her on skates, and keeping her balance. It was clear that fossils like his aunt weren't expected to actually skate. "It's just like riding a bike," she told him. "Once you learn, I guess your body doesn't really forget."

Her body didn't really remember quite as well as she'd thought once she hit the slick concrete. Her legs felt even longer and more awkward than usual, but at least they didn't come out from under her.

Brittany's did, several times, before she got the hang of it. But she giggled while she picked herself up and cajoled Brian into holding her hand once around the rink to give her balance. After one revolution, she let go of him and tottered off on her own, wobbling a little, but upright.

"That's my girl," Lacey murmured to herself. She watched Britt gather speed, single off-center ponytail bobbing as she went around the rink. Brittany's self-reliance always amazed her. She faced the world head on, no matter what the situation. Lacey was so busy watching her, hair glinting golden under the lights, hoping she didn't fall, that she almost ran into the back of another skater.

Lacey skidded to keep from running into him. Her heart pounded, and she was shocked to discover that it wasn't just nearly running into him that made her pulse rapid. It was what she was nearly running into. Lacey couldn't remember looking at a male figure quite this way in many years.

It was the music, she decided. And the atmosphere of the rink, with all the young couples floating around her, Lacey told herself. What else could be making her go absolutely moony over a stranger's curly dark brown hair? It had to be the rink.

Maybe it was the delicious freedom she felt gliding around the polished surface, almost as if she'd found a magic carpet that was taking away all the troubles and stresses in life and giving her back a freedom that felt like Highland, Illinois, twenty years ago.

Freedom that meant she had two parents and no nieces and nephews and a tall, beautiful, dark-haired sister who was in love with the boy down the street. It had been a wonderful time in Lacey's life, and it was nice to recapture a little piece of it here in the music that throbbed around her and the cool air that rushed by her body as she skated the oval.

Here there were no car wrecks, illnesses, or disasters. There were no clients to call and grouse about what they had to pay the federal government, and no endless seminars on new tax forms. There was just Lacey and the music and the cool, cool air.

The man's companion, who was younger and very boyish looking, said something to him, and he laughed. It was a nice laugh, deep and throaty and full. He turned his head, a lock of hair falling over his forehead, and Lacey got a shock.

She had never seen the man before, but there was a connection when he looked at her. The light stubble across his firm, angular jaw and the sparkling eyes both spoke volumes before he'd even said a word.

Lacey was so intent on watching him that some little glitch in the concrete floor pulled at her feet. One hand windmilled as she corrected her balance, and the motion caught the man's eye. He turned his head fully toward her, that flashing hazel gaze making her gulp. There was a flicker of mischief in his eyes as he looked at her and grinned, and before he turned again he winked straight at her.

Lacey tried not to gasp at her reaction to that simple gesture. A thrill went through her from the pit of her stomach, forcing a choked little giggle out of her. What had that new New Year's resolution been? Ah, yes. Seeking adventure. Lacey Robbins was getting a clear message that if she could be bold enough to introduce herself to this man, she could have all the adventure she had ever wanted. Just from one wink.

Pondering all this, Lacey listened to the voice of common sense in her head as it urged her to run as fast as she could in the opposite direction from this attractive man.

She didn't see Brittany until she heard her close in her ear, saying, "Can I have some quarters for the video games?"

Britt was really intent on wheedling. "Skate farther away, honey, and don't hold on to my arm that way," Lacey said, trying to make Britt hear her over the music.

"What?" Britt sidled closer. Her skate slid in between Lacey's, and she grabbed her hard, catapulting them both into the backs of the pair in front. There wasn't even time to warn the winker or his friend before they collided. The four of them all went down in a heap, and in a moment a rink employee in a referee's striped shirt skidded to a stop behind them, directing traffic as they unsorted their various arms and legs from the pile.

Lacey couldn't see for the curtain of honey gold hair in her face. She was suddenly aware of her clothing in a way she hadn't been in years, wondering why she was wearing old khakis and a cotton shirt that had been washed into softness. Britt wiggled nearby, extracting her tail of hair from the melee. Lacey assessed the damage. Nothing seemed to be broken, although a few spots hurt. The worst of it was that somewhere out on the floor were her glasses.

"I hope my glasses are still in one piece, Brittany Kaye," Lacey said sharply. "Nobody else can drive home."

"I could," said a deep voice as parts of a muscular body untangled themselves from around her. "But I believe these are in one piece anyway."

Without her glasses, Lacey couldn't see much. But she still had the rest of her senses, and they were going crazy. Surrounding her were the natural scents of a clean, healthy masculine body overlaid with spicy, crisp cologne that made her think of the park after a rain.

Her own heart thudded in her ears from his nearness and the aftermath of the crash. Strong hands with callused thumbs turned her head a little to each side and back.

The blur around Lacey melted into sharp focus as he slid on her glasses. The first thing she noticed was the stranger's eyes, deep green swirled somehow with bronze. He made sure her glasses were correctly perched on her nose before he withdrew his hands. "All right?"

"F-fine," Lacey stammered, trying to figure out how to stand up. She pushed her hair out of her face. Why was he still looking at her that way?

"Nothing broken or anything?"

It was impossible for her to form coherent sentences with those warm, alert eyes looking at her so intently, so Lacey just shook her head.

"Good."

He was in a crouch on the rink, skates firmly under him when he grasped both of her hands and pulled her to a standing position. As he helped her up, her attention focused away from those hazel eyes and onto the rough-hewn gold cross on the heavy chain around his neck. In that moment it was the most beautiful thing she had ever seen.

Funny, she didn't remember being bumped on the head. As far as she knew, his head hadn't hit the floor either, but his reflexes had sure slowed down. Why else was it taking so long for him to release her fingers? He was still so close she could almost count his long, dark eyelashes. The kind Mom always said were wasted on men, but to Lacey this was anything but a waste.

She tried to think of something to say. "I'm all right now, I think. Thanks…"

"Jack. Jack Dalton," he said, still holding her hand. "And my partner in crime here is Eric." The teenager flashed Lacey a smile while he finished righting Brittany, who looked sheepish but not hurt.

"Lacey Robbins. And my niece, Brittany Horton. And my nephew, Brian Horton, and my other niece, Becca Horton." The others had slid to a stop around the group when they saw Lacey and Britt getting up.

"You okay?" Brian asked protectively. Standing this close to Jack, he looked like exactly what he was, a skinny ten-year-old. But his chin stuck out in determination to take care of Lacey and his sister if they needed it. Jack put a hand on his shoulder, smiling.

"I think she'll be better if we get her sitting down for a little while," Jack said, starting to skate toward the benches. "How about you, Brittany?"

"I'm okay. I'm going to go play video games for a while anyway," she said with a smile. Lacey skated off the rink and gingerly reached into her pocket for two quarters. The motion brought new little zings of pain. A few other things had been bruised along with her dignity. She handed the money to Brittany, who zoomed off.

Somehow everyone except Jack evaporated too. Brian had left once he was reassured that his aunt and sister were both in one piece, and Eric had seemed to perk up the minute Becca was introduced. They skated around the rink together, talking as they skated. Lacey's alarm bells went off at the sight of her niece skating with a strange young man and being as animated as she was. But then she looked back at Jack. He seemed to be keeping a pretty tight rein on Eric. Perhaps she didn't have to worry.

It did feel good to sit down, even on the hard wooden

bench. Lacey sank onto it gratefully, finding just the right angle to avoid the worst spots on her bumped posterior. In a moment Jack was back, carrying two sodas. "I hope you're not an attorney," he said, holding one of them out to her.

She laughed at the sincerity behind the statement, and the concern that lined the spot between his straight dark eyebrows. "Hardly. Besides, I bumped into you. You're not an attorney, are you?"

"Not anything close. I run a jewelry store."

"Dalton's on Park Avenue?"

"That's the one. I'm flattered that you know it." His mouth turned up in pleasure, and Lacey was intrigued by the warmth of that smile.

"I've been there. Do you do your own design work?"

"Every bit," Jack said, his eyes gleaming.

"Does that mean you made that gorgeous cross I noticed around your neck?"

"Of course. I wouldn't wear somebody else's stuff." He gave a short laugh. "Although a cross is definitely somebody else's stuff, isn't it? I'm proud to wear that, though."

"Because you made it?" Lacey challenged, taking a sip of the soda and watching the smile that made it all the way to his flashing eyes.

"Because of whose it was first. Could I make you one?"

"That's nice, but that one looks out of my price range," she said. "I guess I've got too much financial training to be anything but practical. And gorgeous jewelry is not all that practical, at least not for a CPA."

Jack looked very interested. "A CPA, huh? You have a business card on you?"

"Probably," Lacey said, trying to ease her billfold out without standing up. There was one card left, and she handed it to him.

"Can I call you Monday?"

Lacey wasn't sure if this was a business proposal or something more personal. "Sure. Why?"

"I don't have a full-time business manager for the shop right now, and I need some advice." Jack relaxed on the bench. "Really I need more than advice. I need help. The books are a mess."

"I do mostly tax work, but I'd be glad to help you out if I can, Jack," Lacey said. The oddity of the conversation was making her light-headed. Here she was, mentally trying to convince herself that this wasn't the handsomest man she'd seen in years. Even more important, she was trying to deny that there was an attraction between them that far surpassed anything physical. They had said so little, and still there was a connection she couldn't deny. At the same time she was exchanging business cards and talking taxes. If Becca saw her doing that, she'd go home with a paper bag over her head.

Lacey tucked Jack's card into her wallet and closed it quickly so she wouldn't stare. Jack seemed to be doing enough of that for both of them. It wasn't a stare exactly, just a warm, intense look that spoke without words. This was not the way most people assessed business associates, and Lacey willed herself not to blush.

Brittany broke the spell by skidding to a halt in front of them. "My quarters are gone. I lost," she said, her mouth splitting into a grin that showed her missing front tooth.

"You seem more cheerful about it than I would be," Jack said, laughing. His laugh was so infectious that Lacey felt like joining him every time she heard it. Britt seemed to like it too, grinning again and shrugging one shoulder upward.

"Yeah, well, I lost better than usual. This time I blew up three guys before they got to me."

"Ugh," Lacey said, grimacing.

"Aunt Lacey doesn't like video games. She says they rock your mind."

"Rot, darling," Lacey said. "Do you want a soda before I go back to skating?"

"Yes, please. Aunt Lacey, is this an adventure?"

Lacey rose to get her a drink. "I think so."

Britt turned to Jack. "Aunt Lacey's seeping adventure. She told us at lunch."

"Oh, is that so?" There was a definite glint in Jack's eyes. "That sounds like a challenge."

Lacey kept willing herself not to blush. "That's *seeking* adventure, Britt. And you made a resolution to…"

"Keep secrets. Oops. Was that supposed to be one?"

"I think so," Jack said gravely.

Lacey could feel the color rising in her face at the thought of Jack knowing her secrets, any of them. If she left him in Britt's company long, he'd know plenty. It was time to get Brittany a soda and send her on her way. Lacey skated away, though more to regain her composure than to fetch the soda. When she came back to the bench with it, she was surprised to see Jack still there, listening intently to a long description of Brittany's latest monster-bashing escapade with the video games.

"All right, plenty already," she said, handing her the cup. Brittany settled down on the bench to drink, and Lacey headed back toward the rink.

Jack stood up and followed her. "Going back so soon?"

"Just like falling off a horse," Lacey started. "You've got to get back on quick…."

When she got to the edge, the music stopped and the lights dimmed. "Couples only. This skate is couples only," the voice over the public address system blared. "That means two girls,

25

or a girl and boy. No skating backward, no jumps, couples only…"

"Want to skate couples?" Jack took her hand and glided onto the concrete. "I promise, I won't even try to skate backward. Come on, it will be an adventure. And you're supposed to start seeping some, remember?" The music began again, slow and hopelessly romantic. Jack held on to her hand and drew her onto the rink.

Three

The lights were very low, and the music was a slow, gentle throb. Jack stood looking at Lacey, willing her to find a reason to turn him down. That would keep him from making a colossal fool out of himself, and he could just go home instead of standing here. What was he getting himself into?

This was a woman in every sense of the word, including a large dose of mystery behind those tortoiseshell glasses, and she scared him silly. But she also drew him like a magnet. When she began to skate next to him around the rink and he took her hand, it was almost a relief.

It was a very nice hand. Soft and smooth, a little cool, as if she were as nervous as he was. Maybe that was possible. Maybe she wasn't really as serious and put-together as she looked behind those frames. If not, she was putting on a good show. He tightened his grip, then took her other hand so that they were almost shoulder to shoulder. The closer Jack drew her, the better it felt.

He willed her silently not to pull away. There had to be a way to keep her close. He adjusted his movements to hers ever so slightly so that they glided around the oval together. It didn't take much adjusting. Lacey had a natural grace that allowed her to match his movements even though she'd never skated with him before. And Jack already felt as if he didn't want to remain strangers long.

Lacey seemed to be looking at him hard. Then her lovely face broke into a smile that didn't look much older than her youngest niece's. "This is more fun than I thought it would be. You make it look easy."

"Maybe so. I've never done this before," he said as they rounded a corner.

"Gone skating? You seem like a natural." She looked up at him so earnestly. Jack liked the way she looked at him, and he squelched a desire to push those glasses up higher on the bridge of her nose. Even without doing it, he could imagine how her skin would feel under his fingers, satin smooth at the bridge of her nose, where there was the barest shadow of pale freckles.

He caught a glimpse of Eric's red head and Becca's deep blond one as they skated slowly near the side of the rink. Surely Eric was having an easier time of it than this. "No, I've been skating before. My brother and I used to go skating when we were kids, and Eric likes to spend an afternoon here once in a while. I mean I've never skated the last song—skated couples with someone."

"Not even when you were a kid and came with your brother?" Lacey asked.

Jack shook his head. "Especially not then. Jamie and I were too cool for that sort of thing. Unlike Eric, who believes that is the purpose of coming here. Usually I lean against the wall and watch Eric."

"Are you two related? You don't look much alike, but then I don't look much like all of my sister's kids either, do I?"

Jack shook his head.. "No relation. I'm in a big-brother program at my church. Eric's my 'little brother' through the program."

"That's a nice thing for you to do," Lacey said.

"Hey, I'm only taking one kid who isn't mine skating. You're taking three." Lacey seemed about to say something, but Jack continued on. "I'm really glad you did, though. I mean, it's not every day a desperate type like me finds a good accountant."

Her expression was somewhere between a smile and a grimace. "How desperate are you? And how do you know I'm good?"

She had him there. He chose to answer the second question and gloss over the first, at least for now. "I don't. But if you can keep books, you're better than I am, and I'll take it." Jack suddenly had a mental image of Lacey sitting in the chair next to his desk. It was a nice image.

The kids skated by them. Becca was ahead, zipping in front of an interested-looking Eric, who was scrambling to keep up with her. Lacey laughed.

"Eric has good taste," Jack said succinctly.

Lacey nodded, an action that made her glasses slip down again. "I'd say so. I'm pretty proud of her, when we're speaking to each other, that is."

"I'd forgotten for a while before I met Eric just what being a teenager was like. We lost my younger brother a year ago, and my pastor suggested that being a 'big brother' to another young man might help me. After a few weeks the teenage thing all came back in vivid detail." This woman brought out a strain of honesty in him he had thought was gone. "At least after we go out for a burger this evening, he goes his way and I go mine. Being a 'big brother' this way suits me fine. When he bugs me, we part company. His mother has him twenty-four hours a day, seven days a week."

"And probably enjoys it most of the time," Lacey said, her eyes flashing. Whoops. Jack suddenly felt like he was holding hands with a mama tiger. What could he say to get her to sheathe her claws?

"I'm sure his mother is perfectly satisfied," Jack said. "I'm still glad it's her."

Lacey didn't say anything else, but she didn't pull away

either. Jack counted that a point in his favor. He could lie to her and tell her he loved kids and wanted them around twenty-four hours a day. But if she was going to go over the books, Lacey was going to discover that just wasn't so. Why start lying now? Lacey didn't look like the kind of lady who would take that kindly. Eric and Becca skated past them, having an animated conversation, and Jack smiled over at Lacey.

"I'd say I taught him everything he knows, but he's probably taught me as much about myself as I've taught him about anything." He squeezed her hand softly, and her arm brushed against his chest. Jack told himself that it just wouldn't do to pull her up close, facing him, in the middle of the rink. Not when they had met only half an hour before. Restraint was getting more difficult surrounded by the scent of her perfume.

Mercifully the music ended and the lights came up. Jack hoped maybe now his pulse would slow down a little and his body would stop trying to break into a sweat. Before he could regain his composure, Lacey's youngest niece and nephew skated over to them.

"We can't find Becca," Brittany said. The girl looked worried.

Lacey reached down to smooth her hair. "No problem. She's with Jack's friend Eric, remember? We'll find her."

She looked around the cavernous rink, scanning it for Becca. Jack looked with her, wondering where the kids had gotten to. They had passed them not three minutes ago. How far could they have gotten in that time? And why?

Finally, on a third look around the rink, he had his answers. In the corner farthest from them, farthest from anyone, hidden in a shadow, were Becca and Eric. And the "why" of their disappearance was evident. Arms entwined, their lips couldn't have been closer together if someone had used superglue.

Lacey whirled on him, all her earlier friendliness gone.

"That young man is your responsibility, Dalton. So call him off." She skated off the rink, Brittany's hand in hers, Brian following.

"He's not mine, Lacey," Jack called after her. And Eric was going to be very thankful that was the case when the lecture started in the car. Right now he almost wished the goofy kid were his. He could pick him up and shake him by his leather jacket a few times. Skating toward the pair that was finally breaking up, Jack rehearsed what he was going to say.

At least Eric and his stupidity had saved Jack from asking Lacey out on a date on the spot. The thought of a first date with four kids along made him break into a heavier sweat than skating with her in the dark had. There would be time later, when Eric was at home with his mom and her three charges were back with whomever they belonged to. Once he cleaned up this little mess and gave her a day or two to calm down. Now it was time to make a quick exit.

Lacey began taking off her skates, wondering how to handle this. She remembered doing things just as dumb when she was a teenager. All those arguments with her father flooded back in a flash. Staying out past curfew, sneaking away from friends' houses to date boys he didn't like, even once going to a party where the police had been called because of alcohol use. How many of those incidents had there been before her fed-up, single-parenting father had shipped her off to her big sister?

Now she was the one in charge, and it was her turn to do the talking. And she had to find a way to do it that wasn't going to alienate Becca even further, while she brought home to her the serious nature of what was happening.

Help, Lord! she prayed silently. *I can't do this alone.*

~ ~ ~ ~ ~

Becca skated back looking sullen and defiant. "Do I have to say anything?" Lacey asked her.

"Guess not." Becca skated past her aunt and flopped down on a bench to undo her skates. At the other end of the rink, Lacey could see Jack talking to Eric. The boy was flushing at something the older man said to him, coloring almost as red as his hair. Lacey hoped Jack was tearing into him good.

Eric shrugged his shoulders and came over to Lacey and Becca. "I'm sorry, Ms. Robbins. And Becca. Jack says my behavior was inappropriate."

"He's right," Lacey said. "And I'll be happy to accept your apology." Might as well let him leave with shreds of his dignity intact anyway.

Lacey watched them go, noticing the way Jack smoothed his dark hair. When they were about five feet away, Jack stopped and turned back to her.

"I'm really sorry about this. But I can only take so much responsibility for a kid I'm with five hours a week, tops."

Lacey started spluttering, "You'd better be responsible, mister. If he were mine, I'd expect you to be responsible for him while he was with you."

Jack grimaced. "For some things, yes. But, Lacey, he's a fifteen-year-old boy. He's grown up enough to claim responsibility for his own actions."

Lacey still felt like going off like a rocket. "Well, they were pretty crummy actions, if you ask me."

"I won't argue with that," Jack said. "However, let me remind you that it takes two to tango. Or kiss. Especially like that."

Without waiting for a reply, Jack turned and followed Eric.

He had gone about five feet more when he shifted his attention back to Lacey. "Admit it. There for a while this was an adventure, wasn't it?"

"I guess so," she admitted. "And look where it got me." She couldn't shake the nagging feeling that this man was dangerous, at least for her. In her hand, the skates felt like they weighed a ton each. And walking was strange and somehow clumsy after gliding around the rink. Surrounded by her chattering family, Lacey watched Jack catch up with Eric. They put on jackets and strolled out of the rink together, looking very much a pair. She was so intent on watching them that it took a moment for the voice beside her to sink in.

"I said, are you going to see him again?" Becca asked, sounding breathless.

"I doubt it," Lacey said. "After that little display, the last thing I'd want is for you to see his buddy Eric."

Becca groaned. "I know. It was really stupid. But he's so cute. And we started talking, and then…"

Lacey snorted. "The talking isn't what worried me, Becca. What were you doing? No, scratch that. I know what you were doing. But why?"

Becca looked dazed. "I don't know. Something just…came over me."

If the same sort of something hadn't come over her when she had looked at Jack, Lacey would have snorted again. "Well, try to keep it from coming over you again, okay? That is not the kind of behavior I expect from you. We'll talk more at home."

She turned in her skates and gathered everybody to leave. By now Becca was looking embarrassed and repentant. "I'm really sorry, Aunt Lacey. Honest. I hope it didn't mess things up for you too much."

"What do you mean?" Lacey asked, shooing everybody out the door into the parking lot.

"With Jack. I mean, if he was going to ask you out or something..."

Lacey shook her head. "Not likely. I think he just wanted to talk business."

Becca's eyes widened. "Business! Aunt Lacey, the most handsome older guy I've ever seen picked you up off the floor, and all you did was talk business?"

"Yes, business, and what's this 'older' stuff? Neither of us is ready for the rocking chair yet."

"Oh, come on, Aunt Lacey, he's twenty-nine. That's pushing thirty, for goodness' sake. He's nearly twice as old as Eric."

"Thank heavens," Lacey said, shaking her head.

"Are you really just going to see him on business?" Becca said again, sounding almost wistful.

"C'mon, Becca, they're adults," Brian said, picking up his skates and heading over to turn them in. "Adults don't melt over each other in the middle of a concrete floor, like some other people. Oh, Eric," he mimicked in a falsetto, moving fast to get out of his sister's way.

"I hope he comes back," Brittany said. "I liked him anyway."

Coming from Brittany, it was the ultimate sign of approval. Talkative and outgoing with her family, she was usually reserved with everyone else. She definitely didn't go around making snap judgments after one meeting.

"Don't hold your breath, Britt," Lacey said. To herself she had to admit she hoped he would come back, just to apologize for Eric's behavior. Jack might be gone, but his cologne still lingered around her, reminding her of him. "Right now let's go home and fix dinner."

The debate in the van over what to have and whose turn it

was to help cook drove most of the thoughts of Jack Dalton out of Lacey's mind. It was only later, when the kids were cleaning up after the meal and Lacey sat in the living room with a book in hand and the cat on her lap, that she could think of him again.

"I think he will turn up again, cat," she murmured, stroking the soft fur. As she stroked idly, the cat kneaded her lap in contentment. "I hope he will anyway." *Just not too soon,* she found herself saying silently. If Jack Dalton was her chance to seek adventure, he was plenty, even in small doses.

Four

I f she had known how soon Jack was going to turn up, Lacey would never have worn those particular jeans on Sunday. After getting everybody to church, then home and fed, she had felt like crashing for a while. Pumps and pantyhose, her nice dress, everything was shed for the most disreputable jeans she owned and a T-shirt.

She had planned on a quiet afternoon in her office. And it was as quiet as things usually got around the house on a weekend. Becca finished her homework to the beat of something obnoxious on the CD player in her bedroom, and downstairs Brian and Britt squabbled and played video games.

Lacey rolled her shoulders back and stretched, trying to lose some of the stiffness she had acquired while sitting at the computer for two hours finishing up a client's report. The volume level was rising from the family room, and Lacey started down the stairs to tell them to knock it off. Halfway down the stairs the doorbell rang, and she changed directions to answer the door before she broke up the fracas.

She swung the door open, ready to tell whoever was there that she wasn't interested in buying cookies, pizza, raffle tickets, or whatever else they might be selling. There stood Jack, and he didn't seem to be interested in selling anything. His mirrored sunglasses were pushed up on top of his curly dark hair, and he smiled at her.

"Hi. I was in the neighborhood, and I know you're probably still ticked at me, but I decided to stop by. I know it's your day off…"

"No, that's all right. Come on in," Lacey said. She opened

the door wider and smoothed her hair back from her face. At least she had caught it up in a band before she started working on the report, and it felt like it was in relatively good shape. As she backed up, the cat twined around her ankles, and she shoved him gently out of the way with her foot.

"Oops—move," she said. "No going outside. Can I get you something to drink, Jack?"

Jack broke off his perusal of the living room. Lacey hoped that to an outsider it didn't look as cluttered as she was afraid it was. "Hmm? No thanks, I just finished lunch."

"Okay. Mind following me to the kitchen, then, for a glass of iced tea? I haven't finished lunch or even started it, and I'm thirsty." Jack smiled and waved her in front of him, and they went down the hallway.

At the family room she poked her head in the door. "End the argument. Now. We have company. You guys remember Mr. Dalton from yesterday?"

Both children quieted down and nodded. "I do," Brittany said with her most charming smile. "Are you going to have an adventure with Aunt Lacey, Mr. Dalton?"

"Brittany!" Lacey and Brian both chorused. Brian rolled his eyes in disbelief, and Jack coughed.

"Mr. Dalton is here to talk about business, Britt," Lacey said sharply.

Britt giggled. "Oh. I thought he was going to talk about what Eric and Becca were doing...."

"That discussion has been finished. Why don't you two find something to do outdoors?" Lacey hoped her look conveyed that it could be anything that didn't involve being hit by a truck—as long as they went outside.

Britt shrugged and turned, and after another brief look at Jack, Brian followed her. The door slammed shut behind them, banging for maybe the twelfth time since dawn. Lacey didn't even notice.

Jack looked like he was in the twilight zone. Lacey had to concede that perhaps Brittany and siblings could be a bit much for someone not used to the noise and mess and inevitable questions children bring. After this much time in residence, it didn't bother her. Jack seemed to be nearly levitating every time a door slammed. Oh, well, it couldn't be helped. Jack would either adapt or flee. She crossed to the kitchen and poured herself a glass of tea.

"Sure I can't get you one? We even have fresh mint."

"Why not?" Jack watched the children through the kitchen window. "You're really going above and beyond the call of duty here, aren't you? When do their folks get back?"

The question brought the spiral of feelings she had thought were gone by now. "Never," Lacey said bluntly, thrusting the tea glass at him. "I'm it."

Jack looked confused. "Maybe the noise in here is affecting my brain. Did you just say 'never'?" Lacey nodded, and he still looked mystified. "But I thought you were their aunt."

"I am. Their parents were killed in a car accident three years ago. I'm their guardian. I care for them all the time. I feed them, clothe them, and keep a roof over their heads." Her voice sounded a little flat, even to her, and she could feel the tight compression of her lips.

This would be it. He would now thank her very politely for the tea, choke it down, apologize about Eric, and head for high ground. Not that there was any real high ground in central Florida, but Jack would try to find it, just like Sam before him. Lacey counted the seconds as she watched him take a long swallow from his glass.

"That's a lot of responsibility," Jack said, blowing her image of him. He took another long drink of his tea. "But I think there's still room for adventure here."

She started to open her mouth to say something, but before she could, the telephone rang. "I've got it," Becca screamed over the volume of the music upstairs while thundering out into the hall to grab the extension. A moment later there was a screech. "It's Brooke, Aunt Lacey!"

Lacey felt a surge of excitement flow through her. She put down her glass of tea and moved quickly past Jack, wishing there were time to explain. "Hey, guys, Brooke's on the phone!" she shouted into the backyard.

There was a general stampede. Jack withdrew to a kitchen chair, getting out of the way. Lacey gave him points for intelligence, or perhaps just self-preservation. Lacey left the back door open while she grabbed the telephone, hoping to get a few words in before she had to relinquish it.

Becca was giving Brooke the full details of the incident at the rink, an account Lacey could hardly explain with Jack sitting two feet away from her, dodging small bodies as they ran in to talk to their sister. She noticed that Becca conveniently left out the last part about Eric. The door slammed again, and Jack winced. Lacey told herself that maybe the noise level *was* high if you weren't used to it. Oh, well, if he was going to hang around here, he'd better get used to it. She put a hand over her ear so she could hear Brooke.

"Wait. Yes. Let me get a pencil," she told Brooke after hearing that the dorm suite had a new phone number. She motioned for Jack to hand her one that was on the kitchen table among a few glasses and crumpled napkins. He complied and sat back in the chair far away from the traffic. Brooke kept them all amused with stories of her first day back after Christmas break. Lacey even got a few words in edgewise between all the kids talking to their sister and arguing among themselves.

"So, this Jack Dalton guy Becca's been telling me about? He going to hang around long enough for me to meet at Easter?" she asked. At first Lacey panicked a little. Then her eye caught Jack lounging in a kitchen chair, a shaft of sunshine falling on his hair. It gave it rich brown highlights that made her smile. "It's a distinct possibility," she said to Brooke and could almost hear the surprise in the silence at the other end. "But we're costing you a lot of money. Write pretty soon, okay?"

"Okay. I love you all," Brooke said. There was a chorus from all the extensions in the house.

"I love you too," Lacey said before she hung up. She put the receiver back in its cradle. Jack seemed to be regarding her a little strangely. Maybe other women of his acquaintance didn't perch themselves on kitchen countertops while they talked on the telephone. Maybe they didn't, but Lacey did. It was comfortable up there. She slid down and smiled apologetically. "That was their sister. My other niece, Brooke. She just went back to Atlanta for her second semester of college."

"Are there any more?" Jack asked weakly.

"Not unless you count the three locked in the attic," Lacey snapped, then laughed as Jack automatically looked up.

"Sorry," he said. "I guess it's none of my business."

"It isn't, but there are only four of them. Forgive me for snapping," Lacey said. The cat had been prowling hopefully all the time they were in the kitchen, and now it twined itself around her ankles. "Oops, move!"

"Did I catch you at a bad time?" Jack asked softly. "You seem upset."

Lacey looked puzzled, then realized Jack was looking at the cat. "No, that's his name. Oops. I called him something worse when I kept stepping on him in the dark when he was a kitten, but Brooke changed it to Oops, and I guess it stuck." She laughed, and Jack joined her. It was a good sound, as rich and full as it had been the day before at the rink.

"So you're not upset?" Jack asked.

"Who, me? I always get this way when strangers catch me in ragged jeans on my day off, surrounded by clutter and crabby children."

"I'm sorry." He really looked it, too. Those hazel eyes full of highlights were going to be Lacey's downfall if he stayed around. "I didn't know I was going to be stirring you up by coming by."

"You haven't, not that much," Lacey said automatically. It was not quite the truth, but it was easier than telling him everything and letting down her guard. "Since I work here, my home is sort of an extension of my office, and you seeing it all this way, with folded laundry, and the kids' usual stuff in the kitchen isn't the impression I like to make. For most clients I do better than this." She felt better once she had admitted that. She covered the flush the admission caused by pouring herself a glass of tea. "Want to go hide in my real office?"

"I thought you'd never ask," Jack said. The warmth of his smile almost melted the ice in the glass Lacey held as she led him upstairs.

In the office with the door closed, Jack looked around intently. He seemed to be a detail-oriented person, which made Lacey wonder why his books were a mess. The noise from the rest of the house dulled with the door shut, and the office looked very professional. Lacey knew that many of her clients were upset enough, having gotten one of those "we're here to help" letters from the IRS, even before they ever saw her, so she kept the environment friendly.

Everything was done in neutrals, sand and gray, with plants providing most of the color. The furnishings were simple, and all of it blended into an environment Lacey hardly noticed anymore. Jack seemed to be taking it all in.

"I like it," he said finally. "Simple, quiet, kind of peaceful. Just the opposite of my office."

"Oh?" Lacey said, intrigued now.

"Yeah, mine looks like the black hole of Calcutta most of the time. Rotten lighting, papers all over, a few design projects spread out, and the walls still painted the same bilious green they were when my parents moved in sixteen years ago." He laughed at the visible shudder that went through Lacey at his description.

"That sounds...positively revolting," Lacey admitted. "How do you ever get anything done in there?"

"I try to avoid it as much as possible," Jack told her. "Which is why I'm hiring you. Life is too short, at least my life, to mess with that stuff too long."

Lacey's eyebrows shot up. "Hiring me? Who said I'd work for you?"

"Even after that mess with Eric, I was hoping you'd say you would, Lacey," Jack said. "I really did talk to him on the way home. Most of the way home. I don't think he knows what hit him."

"Neither does Becca," Lacey said, her lips pressed thin. "And I don't want her to find out either."

"Does that mean we can't do business?" Jack asked. He had a hopeful, speculative look that gave Lacey another one of those warm feelings. "Admit it. You actually like the thought of untangling my knotty financial affairs, don't you?"

It was hard for Lacey to decide which she liked more, the thought of taking Jack's books apart or the thought of Jack leaning over her chair while she did it.

These thoughts were not businesslike, she reminded herself. These thoughts could lead to trouble. "I guess I do like the idea," she had to admit. "But if we're going to be working together, there are going to have to be some ground rules. And the most important ground rule will be that we both ride herd on Romeo and Juliet. Agreed?"

Jack grinned. "Agreed."

They discussed the terms for hiring her and that they would have their first meeting on Wednesday, but Lacey found it hard to keep her mind on the business at hand. It was so easy to watch Jack instead while he talked, seeing the light flash in his eyes and watching them go from green to bronze and back while he told her about his business and his plans. There was that scent around him again that made Lacey have to work very hard to actually hear what he was saying.

"My folks started the chain years ago, with just the one store on Park Avenue in Winter Park. A few years back they moved to Ocala and opened up a smaller store there just to keep busy." He laughed, folding his hands behind his head and leaning back in his chair. "I can't imagine either of them actually retiring, I mean with shuffleboard and the like. It just won't happen."

"And you and your brother ran the store here?" Lacey prompted.

The light in Jack's eyes abruptly flickered out. "Yeah. We had some real differences of opinion on which way to go with it while he was alive. Personally I wasn't sure we belonged in retail the way Jamie saw us, but he was positive. For me alone, design and custom stuff is the way to go, but it wouldn't have supported both of us." He stopped talking and seemed to see something far distant, something that disturbed him. Lacey didn't know how to break into his thoughts without being rude, so she sat quietly for a few moments.

In the quiet she could hear and feel her stomach growling. She glanced at her watch. In her office alone with Jack, time had telescoped, and nearly an hour had gone by. "I'm surprised the kids have let us alone this long, Jack. We can continue this discussion in the kitchen if you like, but I've got to put a meal on the table."

He came back from wherever his thoughts had taken him. "I'm sorry. I've been imposing, coming here on Sunday...."

"Not really. It's nice to have some adult company for a change," Lacey said, smiling and opening the door. "But I've got to feed the crew soon or they'll revolt and storm the door."

Jack laughed, following her. "Are they really that rowdy?"

Lacey shook her head. "Not really. But if I miss a meal, they start foraging for themselves, and the kitchen becomes a disaster area. Becca's the only one who can really cook, and she'd rather not."

Jack nodded. "I've been trying to teach Eric the finer points of omelets the last few weekends. So far he's progressed to cracking eggs and watching them slip down the side of the sink. It's a start."

Lacey rummaged around in the refrigerator, asking Jack an occasional question while she put together a quick supper. It was pleasant to have adult company, especially when the adult was as easy on the eyes as he was. Lounging around her kitchen table she reveled in the sight of the crisp dark curls that begged her to ruffle them the way she did Brian's.

The more he talked as she cut up raw vegetables and arranged them, the more Lacey felt as if she had been hiding in a cave for a long time. That was the only explanation she could find for the attraction she was feeling for him as she listened to him explain about the jewelry business.

Surely most normal women who went out on dates regularly instead of keeping company with teenagers and tax auditors wouldn't have been this stirred by an attractive man stretching out his legs under their kitchen table. Warmth seemed to radiate from him as she brushed by to get silverware out of the drawer and condiments from the refrigerator.

It was then that Lacey noticed that Jack had stopped talking and was looking at her intently. Perhaps her perusal of him had gotten too obvious. She willed herself not to blush as she turned to him. "I've made plenty of sandwiches. Want to stay?" she asked before she could regret the invitation.

He seemed ready to decline, then changed his mind. "Sure. They look good, and I'm a pushover for anything I don't have to cook myself."

He helped her carry silverware, napkins, and condiments out to the screened-in porch at the back of the house, then stood aside as the Horton gang plowed through the kitchen to fill their plates. Lacey was thankful that there was little squabbling and no spilled milk for a change.

No one burped during dinner or discussed topics of conversation usually forbidden at the table, for which Lacey was silently grateful. She sat at the end of the table enjoying the breeze that played through the screens as the sun began to go down outside.

Jack seemed to hold his own during the dinner conversation. He listened politely to one of Brittany's never-ending stories and was able to discuss music with Becca without provoking the looks Lacey usually got when that topic came up. After the meal was finished, he talked Brian into helping him clear the table in exchange for a quick game of one-on-one basketball. Lacey started to protest that he was company and didn't need to bother, but one look at Brian's face stilled her.

By the time Lacey had put away the leftovers and Becca had loaded the dishwasher after a spirited discussion over whether it really was her turn or not, Jack and Brian were both sweaty and panting, bouncing a ball on the driveway. Lacey stood in the doorway, watching them.

Jack had a feline grace about him and appeared to be enjoying the game. He went up for a layup, and she could see that flash of power in him. There was a love of competition there that seemed to fuel him, but he didn't take advantage of his size to bully Brian. Instead they played an easy, bantering game until Jack flung himself on the porch steps.

"You've worn the old man out, Brian," he said, panting. "I'll concede defeat if you'll get me another glass of that tea with mint."

"Okay," Brian said jubilantly, bounding into the house. Jack leaned against the wall, blowing out while he brushed damp curls back in that gesture that Lacey had already come to love.

"Thanks," she said softly. "He misses that kind of thing."

Jack had a strange, unreadable look. "I guess that's important to a little kid, isn't it?"

Lacey nodded. "Yeah. I can go to the school conferences and cheer at soccer games and do math homework, but I'm not much of an athlete. And it makes me feel bad when I can't give him what he needs."

"Nobody can do everything," Jack said, a flat note creeping into his voice. "It's hopeless even to try." His expression cleared as Brian came back with a huge glass of tea, and he gulped half of it quickly, then relaxed again.

The sun had set, and insects began to bat around the porch light Brian had turned on to finish the basketball game. "We ought to get out of here before we're eaten alive," Lacey said.

She stood and tapped Brian on the shoulder. "Homework all done?"

"All except math, and I've only got one page left," he said hopefully.

"Then go in, do it, and shower," Lacey said. "Tomorrow is—"

"A school day," Brian finished glumly. The screen door slammed behind him, but he went. Brittany was already inside somewhere, probably reveling in the new mysteries that reading unlocked. And judging from the noise level emanating from the open windows above them, Becca was in her room with the music on.

Lacey flicked off the porch light as she stood inside the door, hoping to discourage the bugs. Jack followed her in, rattling the ice in his glass. She turned to look at him, struck again by his grace as he crossed the threshold.

Suddenly she had to know the answer to the question that had been bothering her all afternoon. "Why didn't you leave earlier? I'm not trying to get rid of you or anything," she said quickly, suddenly conscious of the way that sounded. "But once most guys know the truth about the fearsome foursome, they don't stay long."

Jack gave her a long, hard look and set his glass down on an end table. "I don't know exactly. I expect I could find another accountant to go over the books at the shop who wouldn't come complete with so many entanglements," he said slowly. "But another accountant wouldn't be you, Lacey. Your kids are right. You need to have more fun."

"And you think you're just the guy to provide it?" Lacey shocked herself with the bite in her voice.

"Maybe. Besides, if I hadn't stayed for dinner, I wouldn't be telling you good night. And if I weren't saying good night now, for the first time, I wouldn't have any hope."

Lacey felt puzzled. "Hope?" she asked.

"Hope," Jack echoed. "That one of these nights I'll know you well enough to kiss you good night when we part. Definitely hope, Lacey."

They both stood, saying nothing, in the dim light of the entry. "Good night, Lacey," Jack said. "See you Wednesday morning."

"Bright and early," she said, feeling dazed, as he went back outside to his car. It was low-slung and silver and reminded Lacey with a pang of her more carefree days. She hoped more than ever that there were lots of people around Wednesday morning. Perhaps that way she could keep her sanity.

Upstairs something erupted that sounded like a pillow fight with a cat caught in the middle of it. Well, maybe she would keep *some* of her sanity anyway. Whatever was left after the rest of the weekend.

Five

Park Avenue looked totally different on Wednesday morning as Lacey walked along the street. Usually she just thought of it as a collection of boutiques and restaurants, a good place to window shop and enjoy the sights.

But today her focus rested on the sign midway up the block where Dalton's Jewelry looked much more prominent than she had ever noticed before. It glowed like a beacon, making her wonder again why she was voluntarily committing herself to work with a man that disturbed her usual calm.

She felt scared and excited at the same time, convinced that God had something wonderful, and perhaps terribly challenging, in store for her. She took a deep breath and ran cool, damp hands down the sides of her jacket and skirt. She'd thrown every suit and business outfit she owned out of the closet this morning because nothing looked right. Her normal navy and gray blazers and boring matching pants and skirts seemed positively drab when she thought of wearing them with Jack watching. Finally she settled on the houndstooth blazer and a dark skirt, still wondering if it was too short.

Lacey paused to check her hair in the reflection of the store's front window. It looked all right, and she looked past the glare at the display laid out before her. It was beautiful. A pool of black velvet had some truly striking pieces of jewelry on top. A heavy gold bracelet caught her eye, and she could picture it nestling in the palm of Jack's hand, with his brow furrowed a bit in concentration while he etched the design into it.

Thinking of Jack Dalton's callused, warm hands, even designing jewelry, was no way to begin a long day of working with him. If she began by thinking of all the little things about him that had been haunting her for days, like the way the skin around his eyes crinkled when he smiled...No, that was no way to start a business day.

The way to start was to march in, declare her presence, and get to work in a businesslike atmosphere as quickly as possible. Lacey pushed the door, liking the sound of the small, chiming bell that announced her entry.

It wasn't Jack who looked up from the counter when she came in. Instead, a gray-haired lady with twinkling blue eyes and a slightly rounded shape smiled at her. "Hi, I'm Leona," she called. "You must be the accountant."

"I am. Lacey Robbins." The older woman seemed so genuinely happy to see her that it was easy for Lacey to stick out her hand for a greeting. Leona's hand was soft and warm with a firm shake, and Lacey felt much more at ease.

"Great. I'll call Jack down," Leona said. She disappeared behind a curtain and reappeared in a moment. "He'll be down in a bit. We caught him in a creative mode, I think. He's still upstairs. Been sketching all morning. Why don't I show you the office?"

"Fine," said Lacey, aware of a little disappointment because Jack hadn't been at the door waiting for her. That was silly. He had a business to run, and she had a job to do. And now was the time to start doing it. She followed Leona past the curtain and into the office space.

It was half an hour before Jack appeared. Whistling and bounding down the stairs, he was as handsome as usual. After examining his business papers for the past thirty minutes, Lacey was more aggravated at him than glad to see him. True, the sight of him pulling red suspenders up on those gorgeous shoulders was a good way to lift her spirits. But even watching him snap the braces into place didn't dampen her aggravation.

"Jack, these books are a mess!" There were papers and charts spread out all over the desk Lacey was using, and she was ready to hurl them all into the parking lot, or farther.

"I told you that before you came, remember? In the middle of the roller rink, I told you point-blank that the books were a mess," Jack said calmly. Why did he have to be so unflappable and look so good in the process? Jack in red suspenders and gray flannels was the only thing better than Jack in blue jeans. But Jack's books were awful.

"I can barely read half these entries. Why didn't you just go to med school, and get it over with?" Lacey pushed a page toward him. Jack leaned over the page, studying the entries.

"Oh, those aren't all mine. Some of them are Jamie's, see?"

Lacey looked at them again, trying to ignore the hand so close to hers and the sharp scent of his cologne. "No, I don't see. The writing looks the same. Maybe worse, if that's possible."

"You can tell the difference even on the ones he didn't initial if you look closely. He closes his fours at the top, and his zeros look more like eights."

"Wonderful," Lacey muttered. "This is going to be a real picnic."

"Want out?" Jack asked, leaning over the desk again.

"No." The speed of her reply even surprised Lacey, but with Jack this close to her face, there could be no other answer. "But I do reserve the right to complain. A lot."

Leona, retrieving a stack of boxes, overheard her and laughed. "Complain as much as you want, Lacey. If we both do it loudly enough, maybe he'll get a business manager and go back to what he does best."

"Which is—in your estimation?" Jack asked, looking at Leona.

"Designing jewelry," she said without hesitation as she crossed the room with the stack of glossy black boxes, then went back to work.

Lacey watched Jack grimace. "She's right, you know. If that's your work in the front window, you have a real talent for design. But your handwriting's the pits, " Lacey said, turning back to the books.

"I know. It's one of the myriad reasons I don't like the business end of this. Designing jewelry is my idea of fun."

"And untangling finances is usually mine, but, Jack, this is ridiculous." Jack rewarded her with a smile and a shrug.

Lacey looked around. Just like the books, the back room was every bit as awful as he had warned her it would be. The area where Jack did his design work was well lit, surprisingly tidy, and filled with all sorts of interesting tools Lacey had never seen before. The large, solid safes were imposing. And the office portion of the room was terrible. It was poorly lit, and the file cabinets overflowed with dog-eared papers. The solitary desk was a battered metal unit that looked as if the entire building had been built around it.

"How can anybody possibly get anything done here?" Lacey said, barely suppressing a shudder. "I'll bet there are palmetto bugs under here someplace." She expected one of the long, black, multilegged horrors to come scuttling out from under one of the stacks of paper at any moment.

"They wouldn't dare. No self-respecting creature would live on this desk," Jack said. "I avoid this corner as much as possible, but I still have the whole place treated for bugs monthly. I've lived here all my life, and I still don't like creepy crawlies."

"Good," Lacey said. "Then you won't object when I squish anything with more than four legs that crosses my path." Even without bugs, this little corner was drab. The cinder-block walls were bare except for a couple of brochures and a calendar that hadn't been changed in nearly a year.

"You must really avoid this place," she said, tracing a pattern in the light coating of dust on the calendar's picture.

"That was my brother's. For him, this really was fun. I'll never understand it," Jack said, the light tone gone from his voice. "This was Jamie's place. I couldn't change it."

With a pang, Lacey thought of boxing up Beth's clothes months after the accident. "I'm sorry," Lacey said softly.

"That's all right. You couldn't know. And I don't spend any more time here than I have to."

"Why haven't you hired a business manager?"

"A lot of reasons," he said, turning his back on the office portion of the room and striding toward the brighter corner. "Not a lot of money, and the hassle of trying to train a stranger for a family business. It was different with Jamie. He truly loved the business end of things, always had. But his filing and accounting systems were his own, and trying to understand them has taken me long enough that I hate the thought of trying to explain them to anybody else."

"Could your parents help?"

Jack shook his head. "They're really semiretired. They moved to Ocala years ago and opened up a very small shop they could run with their eyes closed. Besides, the last year has taken a lot out of both of them. They don't need any more reminders." There was a bleakness in his face that made Lacey wish she were brave enough to cross the distance between them and hug him. It was the same feeling she got whenever Brian got into a fight at school and got the worst of things, and her hand actually lifted before she brought it back to her side.

He broke the awkward silence that hung between them. "How about I get you some coffee? I've got a pot started up in the apartment, and there are more records up there you'll want to see anyway." She nodded, and he led her up a stairway in the alcove to the upper floor of the building.

Here light flooded in from everywhere. There were wooden shutters at the windows, opened to let the sunlight pour into the white-walled room. It was masculine and spare, with a few excellent framed prints on the walls.

The kitchen was a narrow galley, and Jack slipped in to grab two mugs and pour them coffee. Back in the living room, he gestured toward a corner flanked by large windows. There was a wooden table with clean lines, totally empty except for a few file folders, and a comfortable chair.

"This is where I do my real office work," he said, motioning for Lacey to sit down.

"I can understand why," she said. "It's ten times more welcoming than that pit downstairs."

"I usually put it off until we're closed at night, and I can sit here with the windows open and watch the traffic down on the street. And then, if the spirit moves—and usually it does—I go across the street and treat myself to ice cream before I turn in." Through the shutters Lacey could see the ice-cream parlor and imagined what a draw it would have on someone who didn't want to do what he was doing in the first place.

An hour later she was contemplating a sundae herself. The records spread out before her were a mess. There was a pattern here she was just beginning to discern, and it disturbed her. Granted, the records were disordered, but there was more. Someplace in the records she'd gone over during the morning was a message that told her there was more to the problem than just carelessness.

Right now the pattern wasn't popping up. It was just out of reach somewhere, teasing her. Maybe another run through all of the books would tell her more. Shaking her head, Lacey got up for a stretch and another cup of coffee.

She had finished it and was contemplating another while she pored through the papers in front of her when Jack came back. "I think I owe you lunch," he said, looking at the papers strewn out in front of Lacey. "I know I'd told you things weren't in very good shape...."

"And boy, was that an understatement," Lacey said. "About the only thing that could be worse is one of those polite little letters from the IRS saying they want to audit the place."

Jack smiled weakly, and Lacey noticed he was holding a stack of letters and brochures. The morning mail. There was a slim brown envelope on the top of the stack. "Oh no."

"Oh yes." When he was chagrined Jack had a very boyish look about him. This time it wasn't helping. Even one of his winks couldn't have saved this situation.

"You owe me lunch," Lacey said firmly. "A very nice lunch."

La Venezia was more than nice. It was cool and elegant, and Jack usually saved it for very important clients. It seemed just the right place to take Lacey. The waiters and waitresses were prompt but not overbearing, and a pale translucent slice of lemon floated in the water goblet. The white linen tablecloths were immaculate, and most of the staff members greeted Jack like a friend.

Lacey didn't look comfortable. She'd spent a moment looking at the menu, then set it down. "Problems?" Jack asked.

"Not really, unless you count the fact that the prices here for lunch are close to what I spend on groceries for the entire week." Lacey picked up the menu gingerly again as if she were looking for coral snakes.

"Don't get the idea this is my normal way of having lunch," Jack cautioned. "I do take an occasional client here, though. It's worth it in atmosphere alone."

"I'm glad," Lacey said, looking at the menu again. "If there are too many charges from here in those files, the field auditor is going to love you."

"Don't worry," Jack said with a grimace. "Lunch most days is a sandwich at my desk. When I'm in the middle of a good design project, sometimes I look up and realize the morning is gone, the afternoon has mostly vanished, and I'm still sitting at the workbench. Leona says you could run a train through the back room and I wouldn't lift my head if the work was going well."

"That's your idea of fun, isn't it?" Lacey said softly.

"I guess it really is," he admitted.

"So what happens the days it isn't fun?" The look on her face told him she really wanted to know. It would be so easy to tell her that it wasn't fun most of the time right now. Easy, but not helpful.

"If it isn't, I go upstairs and invent a new sandwich or something. Or maybe pop over and have ice cream for lunch." Jack flashed her what he thought of as his best smile, but he couldn't keep it going. He set down his menu and took her hand. "You're not comfortable here, are you?"

Lacey smiled apologetically. "I'm sorry it shows that much. It's just that I keep thinking about what this lunch is going to be costing you, and it gives me heart palpitations."

Jack squeezed her hand, feeling guilty for making her uneasy. "Would you rather go someplace else? I wanted this to be a break for you, not a discomfort."

Her expression was so earnest behind her horn-rims that Jack wanted to hug her. She smiled at him. "No, really, I want to stay. I guess I'm just being silly."

"Now that's one thing I can't imagine you being, Lacey," Jack said, meaning it. "Practical, astute, delightful, but not silly." He reached across the table, tilted her chin with his fingertips, looking directly into her eyes. As he searched deep within her with his gaze, Lacey sat motionless.

"I'd sure like to see you that way sometime, though. Silly, I mean. You're too beautiful to be so serious all the time."

Lacey's blush made feelings surge through him like an electric current. He wondered if many women got kissed in the middle of La Venezia. It might be worth finding out.

Lacey, however, wasn't cooperating. "Somebody's got to be serious," Lacey said, moving her head away from his touch. "If I weren't so serious, where would all you people who need a good accountant be?"

"Point taken," Jack conceded. "For today you can be serious. And I hope you're hungry too. I'm going to have the crab salad. How about you?"

"What's the most expensive?" she said, eyes gleaming. "I'm going to earn it getting ready for that audit."

Six

They were quiet for a while, ordering, then waiting as their food was set before them. Jack hadn't realized how he must have been looking at Lacey until she put down her napkin. "Do I have salad dressing on my nose or something?"

"What? Oh, not at all. Sorry." He reached across the table and picked up her left hand. "I have just been watching your hands. They're beautiful, you know."

She made a motion to pull her fingers away and hide them in her lap. "Oh, come on."

"Honestly," he said, running his thumb over the tips of her fingers. "I see a lot of hands, and yours are gorgeous. Well shaped, nicely cared for, very pretty."

"Thank you," Lacey said, seeming oddly touched by the attention. "Now if you'll give that back I'd like to butter my bread."

"Sure. Sorry." So much for being engaging and smooth again. What could he talk about that would put her back at ease? "So what brought you to Florida in the first place?"

"A battered sports car. I got riffed from a large accounting firm in Chicago, and Beth and Kevin told me to come down here and find a job. They loved it down here, had settled in beautifully at Faith Community Church, where Kevin was the youth pastor. At the time I really wondered why I lost the best job I'd ever had, but later it seemed like God's way of making me part of this family before I needed to step in and take over."

"So you lived here a while before…," Jack began, then realized he had never heard exactly what happened to Lacey's sister and her husband.

Lacey nodded. "About seven months. Beth and Kevin were living in this huge old house the church owned, and there was plenty of room for one more. Often I repaid the favor of them letting me live there by watching the kids for a night or two while they went on youth outings with the kids from church. Sometimes Becca and Brooke would go with them, when the age of the kids on the outing was right. That weekend they both had colds and stayed home."

Lacey looked down at her plate for a moment and sat silently. Jack could see that this was still hard for her, even after several years, and for a moment he was tempted to tell her he didn't need to know. But somehow he did, so he let her collect her thoughts and go on.

"They made it home from a big youth gathering in Jacksonville and dropped all the kids off at church. Coming home they had to get on a state road for a short distance, and that's where the drunk driver hit their van. The police say they probably died instantly. I thank God for that, and the fact that the kids didn't see it." Lacey's eyes seemed to glitter, and Jack found himself putting a hand on top of hers. She didn't flinch or pull away, just continued, lost in her story. "The church gathered around us like a family. Kevin's life insurance paid for a house we could all live in, and I could continue the tax business I'd started. I sold the sports car, bought a van, and here we are."

She sat up straighter, smiling again. Jack marveled at her resiliency. His head was still spinning with unanswered questions. "Don't you wonder why this happened? I still ask God every day why Jamie's gone."

"Of course I wonder," she told him. "Some questions just

aren't going to be answered in this life. Remember, 'now we see through a glass, darkly.' I have to accept that God has Beth and Kevin in his care, and right now my job is to take care of their kids. I'm thankful I was able to live with them for a while to make the transition before it was needed."

Jack found himself pulling his hand away. "I wish I had that kind of faith. I still can't see any good in my situation."

"Somewhere, something positive has to come out of it, Jack. God's always with us in every situation, the bad as well as the good. Maybe you're just not seeing what God wants you to see yet."

"Maybe." Jack's voice sounded flat, even to him.

Lacey gave him a wry look, then turned her head to watch the dessert cart go by.

"We may end up doing this again after the field audit, Jack," she said, eyeing the desserts. He almost thanked her out loud for changing the subject.

"Get me through that, and I'll take you back here, guaranteed," he said. "I might even make it dinner then, depending on what the results of the audit are."

"I'm not a miracle worker," Lacey snapped.

"Is it that bad?" Jack braced himself for questions about the payments to Kimberly. Lacey was astute enough to find those quickly.

"I've only had a couple of hours to start looking things over, but I don't like the way they look," Lacey admitted. "I'll tell you more about it in a day or two."

The waiter stopped beside them, dessert cart in tow.

"I lose my appetite when I'm upset," Jack said, his shoulders sagging a little. "That doesn't mean you should too. You still want dessert?"

Lacey shook her head. "Not today. How about going for a

quick walk up the block instead to clear out some of the cob-webs; then I'll go back to work."

"We both will," Jack said, motioning for the check. "I've got a pendant to finish by Friday that's going to take every minute I can give it." And a check to deliver to Kimberly again, but he wasn't about to tell her that. It was time to get back to business.

Jack was a brisk walker, with a bounce in his step that Lacey found attractive. He seemed to be a gentleman of the old school, determined to stay on the outside of the sidewalk and with her all the time as they walked down the block looking at shop windows.

He glanced at most of them with what looked like professional interest in what others were doing with their windows. Then they came to the cozy secondhand bookstore halfway up the block. He slowed to a walk, then stopped altogether. It seemed all he could do to keep from pressing his nose against the glass like a kid at a toy store. "Something tells me you like books," Lacey said.

"You didn't go into the spare bedroom of the apartment, did you?" Jack said. "One whole wall is fitted with bookshelves. I started counting one time, but I lost count at a little over 500 and gave up."

Lacey gave a whistle. "Yep, I'd say you liked books. Anything in particular?"

"Old books of about any kind, honestly," Jack said, his eyes glowing. "I like the way they look and feel, the quality and weight of them. And I love reading them. It's almost like opening a time capsule when you pick up some of them. Life wasn't always as harried and complicated as it is now, Lacey. There really were simpler times." He gazed down at the volumes in the window. "Now there's a beauty."

He waved toward a heavy two-volume set in glossy brown leather. Lacey strained to read the title on the binding. "Oh, poetry," she said, trying not to show her lack of enthusiasm.

"I guess I have more of that than anything, if I have a specialty," Jack said. "Do you collect anything?"

Lacey grimaced. "Pantyhose without runs. My collection never rises over two, though." She shrugged her shoulders with a smile. It was hard to tell this single, carefree man that collecting anything was a luxury when there were four people who depended on you for food, shelter, and tennis shoes. Lots of very expensive tennis shoes.

She was surprised when Jack turned from the window to walk on. "You're not going in to look at those any closer?"

"Are you kidding? A two-volume set of Browning in good shape is more than I can indulge myself in right now." When he named the figure, Lacey actually gasped.

"That's a joke, right? Nobody would pay that for old books."

"I would, if I didn't have anything else that caught my fancy at the moment," Jack said. "Maybe if I get that pendant done I'll reward myself." He turned and offered his arm, seeming anxious to get back to the shop and go to work.

Lacey forced a smile and walked next to him but didn't take his arm. Touching Jack Dalton would be borrowing trouble. He was beginning to look too much like a knight errant already in his jaunty red suspenders and curly hair ruffled by the wind.

Even as she thought it, Lacey told herself she was being silly. Men who indulged themselves in expensive hobbies and ran their businesses the way Jack apparently did were not knights, errant or otherwise. They fell more into the category of adventurers, definitely looking out for themselves first. That was the last thing Lacey needed, even when the adventurer looked as appealing as Jack.

No, better to treat this as merely business that would resolve itself in a few weeks. She would tidy up Jack Dalton's financial affairs, sit in on his audit, then glide out of his life and leave him with no entanglements, just the way he professed to want it. That way he could keep on sailing along, spending his money on leather-bound sets of Browning, and she could spend hers on leather high-tops. That was the way it was supposed to be.

Except, if that was the way it was supposed to be, Lacey asked herself, why did the mere act of his holding the door open for her as she walked through it make her react this way? He felt it too. She could tell by just watching him. The way his eyes widened into green and bronze depths as he stood there and the bell jangled softly above them was all the proof she needed.

"Just us, Leona," Jack called to the older woman who came out of the back room.

"Good. I've got Mrs. Dunwoody on the phone about that pendant, Jack." He moved quickly for the back room to take the call while Lacey stood, waiting for him in the showroom.

"Did you have a nice lunch?" Leona asked.

"It was very nice," Lacey said.

"Awful pricey, though, isn't it? Jack always takes me there for my birthday. I enjoy it once my breathing regulates." She smiled again, and the skin around her eyes crinkled. Lacey felt like she knew this lady even though she'd only met her this morning.

"Are you going to get things in shape around here?" Leona asked. "Heaven knows it needs to be done. I've worked here since Jack's parents opened the place. It hasn't been the same since the boys started running the shop, especially now. Jamie was always the one who was interested in the business side of things. Jack really needs to find someone to do it on a full-time basis. If he could be left to design jewelry…" She shook her head in awe. "You can't believe what that young man can make."

"I like what I've seen already," Lacey said, motioning toward some of the pieces in the cases.

"Yes, and this isn't even the best stuff. Has he shown you the pendant?"

"Not yet, but I'm about to," Jack said, coming from the back room. "She wants it by noon Friday, so I've got to finish it quick. It seems Mr. Dunwoody is getting some sort of civic award, and she wants to wear it to the ceremony."

"Won't that be a rush for you?" Leona asked.

"Not that bad," Jack answered. "And besides, with what she's paying, we can keep things going for quite a while." He waved Lacey toward the back room. "Come on and take a look at this."

He opened a piece of black velvet onto his work table, switching on the overhead lights. As he did so, a blaze of light gleamed in the middle of the cloth. There was a golden sunburst, with irregular edges and sparkling stones embedded in its surface. It was so beautiful Lacey forgot to breathe.

"That is fantastic," she said finally. The pendant was superb, like nothing she'd ever seen before. Looking at it she had a new respect for Jack even if his books were a mess. Here was beauty she couldn't have created in a lifetime of trying.

"I still need to work with the clasp a little. I'm not satisfied with the way it attaches to the chain. I want to make sure it moves with its own weight but still has enough strength that it's going to stay stable," he explained, turning the piece over. "Look, I'll show you what I mean."

He guided her with a firm grip until she was standing facing the mirrors that lined the store at eye level, set into the paneled and wallpapered walls. Then he unclasped the pendant and draped it around her neck. Jack hooked the clasp, unaware of the emotions that Lacey could see rising in her reflection.

He lifted her hair and let it fall over the necklace on the back of her neck, a gesture so natural that Lacey marveled at it. Her pulse would not slow…with Jack's touch…with his beautiful creation hanging suspended, dull gold and blinking, around her neck. The wish that grew in her that no other woman would get to share this beauty with her was foolish, and she tried hard to push it away.

"See," he said while moving the chain, "it just doesn't move right yet. The clasp is too heavy, and it snags…."

"Ouch, it sure does," Lacey said, bucking backward involuntarily as the heavy thing nipped at her hairline.

"Oh, sorry," Jack said. In a flash his arms left their circle around her and he was lifting her hair, gently, and untangling the necklace. "I didn't mean to hurt you."

"I know you didn't. It's all right." Lacey rubbed the spot where the clasp had pulled. Jack's apology had been sincere, but Lacey could see his attention already focused on the puzzle of fixing the clasp.

"Go ahead and work with that. I've got to go hit the books again," she said, watching the gratitude in his eyes. In a few moments he was leaning over the necklace at his worktable, tinkering with some minute piece of the fastener, lost to the world around him.

Over the dark head bent over the pendant, Leona caught

Lacey's eye with a smile that seemed to say, "What did I tell you?" Lacey cocked her head to motion that she was going upstairs, and Leona nodded and went back to the front of the shop.

Jack may have been a creative genius, but he was a financial disaster. Lacey went over the records from the store more carefully and sighed as she closed the ledgers. Things were disorganized, and under that there were problems. They probably shouldn't be in the business of selling expensive lines from outside suppliers. The sales just didn't justify the cost they were paying.

She leaned back in her chair for a minute, relaxing. Lacey tried to make all the tightness pour out of her tense shoulders. Sitting there, with her eyes closed, she could see the ledgers in her mind's eye, and suddenly she knew.

She riffled through the books for the main store. Tracing payments back for years, there was one entry that was always the same. "And it shouldn't be," she muttered out loud. There was no way that a notation for supplies should come that regularly for exactly the same amount.

Once a month, like clockwork, a check had been cut to Kimberly Thompson for just over four hundred dollars. Lacey traced the payments back for over two years, and they were always the same. It was difficult to tell whether Jack had written them all, but it seemed to be the same awful handwriting. Her tiredness hung on her shoulders like a heavy overcoat as Lacey sat back in the chair again.

This couldn't be happening. Jack was a little irresponsible, maybe. He drove a flashy car and bought expensive little presents for himself. But Lacey felt he was basically honest, even though this particular entry in his books disturbed her.

The check register wasn't on this desk. It was downstairs in the office next to Jack's work area. Lacey went down the stairs, intent on looking at it and then confronting him. When she got there, the back room was empty. Opening the check register, she got a shock. Since lunch there was another check written to Kimberly Thompson. The stub was there, and the check was gone. So was Jack.

Leona stuck her head through the doorway. "If you're looking for Jack, he left about ten minutes ago. Said something about an errand in Sanford. Why don't you go on home and we'll see you in the morning, okay?"

"I think you're right," Lacey said. She went upstairs, her heart heavy. She straightened her makeshift desk a little and put some folders into her portfolio. She looked around the room, so filled with Jack's presence. He couldn't be a thief. It just wasn't possible. Nobody with eyes that warm could be, she told herself.

Still, there was something going on. He'd been concentrating so hard on the necklace he'd almost looked like he was in a trance. And whoever Kimberly Thompson was and whatever Jack paid her for, it was more important than the work that sustained his life. Lacey puzzled all the way home with no success.

By the time she got there, the light was fading. No one greeted her at the door except the cat, who came and rubbed joyfully around her ankles. She smiled at the touch of his sleek fur, glad to have the feeling she'd been missed. She could smell supper cooking in the kitchen and blessed Becca for being thoughtful.

Upstairs as she slipped into jeans and a T-shirt she could hear little electronic noises from her office. Brian sat facing the computer terminal, bent on one of his endless rounds of his favorite game.

"Any luck today?" she asked, ruffling his hair as he sat, serious, before the screen.

"Not much. I won four tournaments and killed the dragon, but then while I was out jousting, Philip the Bold came and sacked my home castle." He slumped in the chair and flicked off the screen so that the noises stopped and the light telescoped in on itself.

"You've got to watch those knights in shining armor, sport," Lacey said softly as she patted him on the shoulder. "Sometimes they'll mow you down instead of rescuing damsels in distress." Even if they did look fantastic in red suspenders, she thought to herself. She went downstairs to finish up the supper Becca had started and hoped none of them asked her how her day had gone. For the first time in years she honestly wouldn't have known what to say.

Seven

Saturday Lacey woke up feeling drained, still wondering if she should go in to Dalton's and confront Jack. If she did, she still didn't know what she was going to confront him with. After working on the records for two days at home, she was more confused than ever.

Most of the books were a mess but easy to untangle. Nowhere but in that one recurring entry was there any indication that Jack, or anyone else, had been doing anything out of the ordinary. Things weren't run exactly the way Lacey would have arranged them herself, but they seemed honest enough.

Still, the nagging sensation that things weren't right dogged Lacey while she nibbled on toast, showered, automatically dished out everybody else's breakfasts. All that done, she sat down for a cup of coffee, hoping to sort out her thoughts. They just wouldn't sort. Shrugging, she loaded the dishwasher, threw a load of jeans in the washer, and gave up.

Thinking about Jack made her head hurt. On one hand he was gorgeous, funny, engaging. On the other, he might be keeping dishonest books, and he was not all that thrilled by the crowd that surrounded her. He was obviously a Christian but seemed to be struggling with his faith. Being around him was an adventure, she had to admit. With Jack around she would be fulfilling her New Year's resolution in spades. Lacey had to concede that she could also get herself in deep and serious trouble.

The trouble wouldn't all be financial. Working around Jack Dalton was reminding her of how lonely she'd been while raising these kids and getting a business going. Lacey was so absorbed in her thoughts that when Britt came up and said, "Well, are we going or not?" she just dreamily answered.

"Sure, let me get my purse." She was already reaching for it and her keys before the jubilant tone of Britt's shriek got to her. Where was it she was supposed to be taking the child? Lacey took a look at her ever-present, all-knowing kitchen bulletin board.

"Oh no," she muttered, following Britt out to the van. Skating lessons at the rink. Britt was already too far gone to call back, thanks to Lacey's woolgathering. Working around Jack was making her into a lunatic. And who but a lunatic spent her Saturday morning at the roller rink surrounded by dozens of short bodies all trying to skate backward?

The din at the rink was unbelievable. Once Lacey got there and got in, Britt got very clingy. "You're going to do it too, aren't you?" Her eyes were so huge Lacey couldn't say no. She stowed the paperback she'd been looking forward to reading in her purse and went to rent skates. Once she was heading for the counter, it sounded like more adventure. Definitely something she could tell Brooke about when she called. The rink manager looked at Lacey a little askance when she asked if she could take lessons.

"We've never had anybody over twelve express an interest before," he said, with a smile tickling his face. "Of course, there's always a first time for everything." With the mood she had been in lately, that was all it took to make her determined to take lessons.

So Lacey, in her sweatpants and T-shirt, wishing for Brian's kneepads and using one of Becca's obnoxious neon scrunchies scavenged from the bottom of her purse to keep her hair out of her face, was learning to skate backward. The only individual she could look in the eye was the instructor, a pleasant woman in her thirties who'd looked bemused when Lacey asked to join the class.

"Sure. Why not? And you can even call me Janice instead of Mrs. H," she said.

Keeping up with these little kids was hard work. They seemed to do most of the things Janice asked them to effortlessly. And they definitely had a shorter trip to the hard concrete floor than Lacey did. After the third time she found the floor, she was beginning to wonder about the wisdom of learning the finer points of roller skating.

Still, once she'd spent the morning wiping sweat out of her eyes and finding muscles she hadn't known existed, there was a wonderful moment that told her she should keep on. It was really, honestly fun. Suddenly the music was playing and she was flying around the rink, forward, then backward, then forward again. She didn't fall—didn't even lose her balance. Instead there was the feeling of long-legged grace she hadn't had since she was nineteen and finally felt that she was growing into her coltish body. She was weightless, floating, and she never wanted it to end.

While she was flying, she knew how Jack had felt Wednesday evening when she'd seen him last, bending over the gold starburst pendant, whistling to himself and oblivious to the world. Janice's whistle cut through her exhilaration soon enough. "That's it for today. Come back next Saturday, everybody."

Janice sought Lacey out as she skated off the rink. "You did a good job. Another couple weeks and I'm going to put you in the advanced class."

"Oh?" It was the only thing Lacey could think of to say.

"Yeah. The students are taller, too. You won't feel so out of place. We may even get you to skate in parades with us," Janice said.

Lacey shook her head. "I'll pass on that, thanks. I'm just doing this to keep Britt company." *And because someone said I ought to be silly once in a while,* she thought.

There had definitely been enough silliness in Lacey's day by the time she turned in her skates. There were muscle aches in locations she hadn't thought possible, and at least one bruise was forming on a very sensitive spot. That would take some coddling on the way home. Her glasses kept sliding down her nose thanks to the sweat she'd worked up, and Lacey knew without looking that her hair had collapsed into a limp hank down her back.

Brittany talked at a velocity known only to her most of the way home. "...And by next week I'm going to scissor backward, even Sheri will do it by then, I think. Do you know the tooth fairy leaves her two dollars for every tooth? Isn't she lucky? Is that Mr. Dalton playing basketball with Brian?" she asked as they pulled into the driveway. "It looks like his car."

Jack's car was on the street, and Jack was in the driveway, going one-on-one with Brian. They'd been at it for a while, judging from the discarded heap of clothing on the porch. They were both down to shorts, socks, and shoes. It was an arresting combination on Jack.

As she stepped out of the van and got closer, Lacey could see that nestled in the hair on his chest was that cross on a thin gold chain. It only served to accent the deep golden tan of his skin and the sparkle of sweat that moved down his neck as he stood, panting and watching her. His eyes were shaded by sunglasses, so she couldn't tell what he was thinking as he looked at her, pulling in a deep breath.

It was easy to know what *she* was thinking—almost too easy. But she pushed the thought away before it led down a path she wasn't going to follow. The thud of the ball on the driveway pulled her thoughts to the concrete driveway under her feet. Jack was here to play basketball with Brian. She'd better stick to thinking about him as a client and perhaps a friend. Lacey swallowed once and brushed her hair off her face. "Hi. You get roped into a game?"

"No, I volunteered," Jack said. "When they told me you'd be back before one, I decided to hang around."

Lacey looked around. "You talked to Becca, too?"

"Sure did. She'd still be out here playing basketball but she broke a nail, so that was the end of that."

Lacey looked at Jack in amazement. "Becca was playing basketball? The child who has never broken a sweat in living memory was out on the driveway actually participating in something with her brother?"

Jack's laugh was short but full. "I told her Eric likes sports." He took off the sunglasses and wiped his face with his discarded shirt, and Lacey could see the gleam in his eyes. "That got her playing quick enough."

Lacey smiled, picturing the unlikely trio playing ball. "I hope you stayed between them."

"Almost all the time."

"So what brings you out this way on a Saturday morning?" she asked, feeling grateful that Jack had stopped playing long enough to put his shirt back on. It made looking at him much easier.

"You didn't say good-bye," he said. "I wondered if something was wrong."

Nothing like being put on the spot. "Kind of, but I don't want to discuss it on the driveway. Besides, that was three days ago. I worked on paperwork here for you about four hours on Thursday and put in another three hours yesterday. Where have you been since Wednesday?"

"Working on the pendant. I decided to take the clasp off altogether and start over. Then I got this great idea for a pair of earrings...." She could see his eyes start to mist over with the fever of creating something else with gold.

"Okay, I think I understand." In an odd sort of way she did. Lacey remembered the concentration he had poured into his work Wednesday night and imagined that it could continue for days. "So how did your client like your pendant?"

"She really liked it. And she wants the earrings when I get them done too," Jack said, beaming. "I'm celebrating tonight—taking Eric out for pizza. That's one of the reasons I came by. I wanted to see if you might be interested in coming along."

"I don't know," Lacey fumbled. "I can't exactly ask Becca to stay home with the kids on such short notice, and the younger two can't be left alone...."

"No, I meant everybody," Jack said, catching her wrist as she moved away from him. "I think Becca could find room for the evening on her busy social calendar, according to what she told me earlier. I didn't intend this as a date exactly. My idea of a good time with a lady doesn't include teenaged chaperones. It's just a celebration, okay?"

Lacey was suddenly aware of just how wretched she must look right now. "Okay." He released her arm then, and Lacey restrained the urge to run inside. When she reached the doorway at the slowest walk she could manage, she turned. "Where and what time?"

"Where do you usually go for pizza?"

Lacey groaned. "Don't ask my kids, or you'll get the trek of the century."

"Oh?" The way his eyebrow lifted like that made her thrill inside just like his winks did. There was a little notch at the outside corner of the left brow that almost begged to be traced with the tip of her finger.

"They're convinced that there's no pizza on earth like you can find at this little Greek place in New Smyrna."

Jack tried not to stare. "That has to be fifty miles."

"Every bit," Lacey said grimly. "So just pick the place, and tell us where to meet you."

"I've got a better idea," Jack said. "I've got to try the best pizza on earth. If we come by about five, can we take the van? We could all go in my car, but it might get a touch crowded."

Just imagining the crowd trying to shoehorn into Jack's car and the effect that would have on Eric and Becca made Lacey very practical. "We'll definitely take the van. And five is fine. See you then."

She leaned on the door after she closed it, breathing deeply. Even in the van it was going to be a long drive sitting next to Jack Dalton.

Eight

There was a lull in the music. Neither Jack nor Eric had gotten up in ten minutes to renew the battle over control of the jukebox, and no one else had put in money either. Jack looked across the table at Lacey, his easy smile making her flush. "You didn't tell me that they also had the world's best Greek salad here."

"A woman's got to have some secrets." Lacey reached for a napkin. "Britt, you have crumbs on your cheek."

With great dignity, Brittany took the offered napkin and brushed away the offending crumbs. "Thank you, Aunt Lacey, I can do it myself." She sat with an air of royalty next to Jack, dressed in one of her fanciest dresses, complete with the necklace she'd gotten for Christmas.

Not once had the chain strayed to her mouth, even when it took fifteen minutes to get their salads and drinks in the busy restaurant. Lacey stifled a giggle. She and Jack might not be considering this outing a date, but nobody had told Britt that. As far as Britt was concerned, the rest of the table was along for the ride during her dinner with Jack Dalton.

She had instructed him on the menu with a gravity only a six-year-old could manage, warning him not to let them sneak furry fish onto his salad or pizza. "They have these spiny things, and they are gray," she said, wrinkling her small nose. "They are totally gross."

"I'll remember," Jack had promised solemnly. As a result, the pizza they were going to share was devoid of anchovies and had extra pepperoni, which he professed to like as much as Brittany did.

The silence was getting to Eric, and he went back to consult the jukebox again. "You're going to blow your whole allowance tonight, aren't you?" Jack said.

"Beats listening to that elevator music you keep putting on," Eric shot back. Lacey watched him saunter to the jukebox. He had cleaned up nicely. His khakis actually looked pressed, and his dark red hair gleamed. Even though she suspected he didn't really need it, he was scented with aftershave.

Becca followed him, leaning on his arm, and Brian went along to peer over the other side of the box. That way, Lacey noticed, he was as far as possible from his sister but still near Eric. Brian's teasing that afternoon had ended abruptly when he'd found out that Eric had led his junior-varsity soccer team to the district finals. Suddenly Eric was a man to be listened to, even if one's older sister was there.

It was a fact that made Lacey thankful. She had seen Becca's elation over going out with Eric, even among this group of people, and it made her feel very old. Becca was too young to start this, the dating, the caring so intensely about growing up and moving on.

If Becca had wanted to listen, Lacey could have told her to stay a child just a little longer. That it was no fun trying to be an adult during your early teens, even though that heady sense of independence felt so good at first. By the time Lacey had turned fifteen, her father had washed his hands of her. Lacey's open rebellion after her mother died had been too much for the quiet, bewildered man to handle.

Of course, Kevin and Beth had been glad to let her live with them and go to high school in Chicago, where they'd settled at the time. Beth welcomed her with open arms, even though Beth already had an active preschooler and a baby to care for. Still, since then Lacey'd been responsible for herself, and it wasn't any picnic. She wanted to scream to the vibrant young girl across the room, giggling while she leaned against Eric, to slow down while she still had a chance.

She felt someone touch her arm and looked back across the table. "Something wrong?" Jack asked, genuine concern in his voice as he kept his hand on her skin.

"Nothing," Lacey lied, but she could tell it didn't satisfy him. "I guess she just looks so young...."

"Don't worry, I'll ride herd on Eric. I'm not about to let him get into anything like that night at the roller rink. His mother would have my hide," Jack said, gently removing his hand. "I'm supposed to be providing a positive role model. I think that means no fraternizing with the enemy for either of us."

"I didn't mean we had to be the enemy," Lacey started. "It's just that...well, I guess I have to realize that Becca's growing up too. First Brooke, now her."

Jack seemed relieved to have another subject to jump on. "So how's life in Atlanta, anyway? Any more phone calls?"

Lacey shook her head. "I plan to call her tomorrow. We usually do most of our corresponding through e-mail, but every so often we need a real call. I think she's a little homesick but fine. Brooke always lands on her feet."

"Just like a cat," Brittany piped up. "Aunt Lacey, if we dropped Oops out a window, would he land on his feet?"

"No," chorused both adults at once, looking at the little blond cherub sitting between them with a calculating expression on her face.

"That is, he probably would, sweetie, but let's not ever find out, okay?" Lacey said. She hoped the pizza would be coming soon. She needed a break from this conversation.

It wasn't too much longer before they were all reaching over each other to get to three kinds of pizza. Eric and Brian favored one that had everything possible (except Brittany's furry fish) on it. Becca and Lacey, the purists, went for vegetarian, and Jack and Britt exclaimed over their pepperoni.

Finally Jack leaned back in his chair, almost moaning. "All right, I give. I cannot eat one more bite." He watched in amazement as Eric and Brian continued to work on their pizza until it was gone. By the time they were finished, everyone else at the table was laughing. Neither of the boys even looked sheepish.

"This calls for a walk on the beach," Jack said, pushing back from the table. "I can't imagine trying to go back until I walk some of this off."

Lacey didn't argue. She felt as full as she always did when they came here, but it wasn't such a bad feeling surrounded by her family. Jack was becoming disturbingly close to fitting into the category of family already, she reflected as they squabbled over the bill.

"I'm getting this, with no arguments," he said, lifting the check away from her.

"But there's only two of you, and four of us, some of whom eat like horses. I can't let you do that," Lacey said, determined to be as stubborn as he was.

"Nope. It's your van and your gas that got us here, and I'm the one that's celebrating, anyway. Let me get it this time." Jack turned and walked to the cashier, oblivious to any more argument.

Lacey shrugged. If he wanted to spend his money that way, it shouldn't bother her. This way there would be more of hers left next week for that trip to the shoe store she had been putting off. The bill for everybody at once always made her queasy.

They drove the few blocks to the public-beach parking lot, and the kids streamed out of the van. In the dark, the waves broke in shimmering lines in front of them. They looked inky black capped with silver, and the kids were all pulling off their shoes to dare each other to wade in the cool January surf.

Eric was still rolling up his pants legs when Becca plunged in, then danced back, shrieking. Lacey looked beside her to see Jack taking his shoes off. "You're going to join them?"

"Of course. Aren't you?"

She hadn't planned to until she watched him shuck his loafers. Then she rolled up the legs of her gray slacks and took off her shoes and socks, feeling the cool sand between her toes. Jack held out an arm, and Lacey took it, glad for his warmth on the cool beach. They ambled along behind the kids, just at the edge of the surf. Here only a gentle rolling wave teased their feet once in a while. After the first one, Lacey began to enjoy it.

"Now, admit that it wouldn't be nearly as much fun to be walking up there on the dry sand with your shoes on," Jack said. His arm slipped around her naturally, and he matched her pace easily. Lacey liked the way their bodies fit together, especially here in this moonlit place between land and sea.

"You're right," she murmured over the breakers. "If you look out toward the ocean, you can pretend you're out in the middle of nowhere instead of on a little strip of public beach. It's very relaxing."

The kids thundered down the beach laughing until they surrounded Jack and Lacey. "So much for relaxing," Jack said as they were engulfed.

"Brian says there's a great ice-cream parlor a block from where we parked the van. Can we go there and meet you later?" Eric asked, pulling on his shoes.

Jack threw back his head and laughed. "You're hungry? Already? No, don't even answer." He pulled his wallet out of his back pocket and handed a bill to Eric. "Go on. We'll be there in a few minutes. I don't think the two of us are quite ready for dessert."

Lacey groaned. "I won't be ready until tomorrow, at least. Britt, you and Brian stay close to the older ones, and no horsing around." She knew there would be at least a little, but she also knew that Becca would keep them in line. She might be rebellious when it was only herself against Lacey, but given her younger brother and sister to watch, she looked out for them well.

"So should we follow them?" Jack asked.

"Eventually. But we can give them a few minutes on their own," Lacey said, reluctant to lose his arm around her and the spell of the water and sand around them.

They turned around to follow the kids toward the parking lot. The children ran, laughing and talking with each other, up the packed sand near the waves. Jack and Lacey ambled along, still at the water's edge, getting farther and farther behind. After a moment, Jack stopped.

"You've got the nicest hands," he said, looking down at the one he held in his. "I know that sounds ridiculous, but I keep noticing that. The first time I picked you up off the rink floor, I noticed them. They're so beautifully shaped." He brought her hand up to his mouth and nuzzled the palm, silencing any rejoinder Lacey was about to make.

She stood there, mesmerized by the touch of his lips on her palm. The contrast between the cool air blowing around her and the warmth of his mouth was stunning.

In a moment her hands were in his hair. Lacey didn't remember moving, but she was very aware of his mouth on hers as the waves curled around their calves. There were colors she'd never seen before blossoming behind Lacey's closed eyelids.

The cool wavelets teased their ankles; then a large wave rocked them, and Jack pulled her closer to balance them both, putting two hands on her back for support as he drew in a long, ragged breath. Their foreheads leaned together, and Lacey wondered if Jack was having as much trouble getting his eyes to focus as she was.

"We're going way past fun here, Lacey," he said, his voice a little shaky. "I never intended to do that."

"No more fraternizing with the enemy?" Instead of the outrage Lacey knew she should feel, there was a painful yearning, knowing he was right.

"That was a really bad choice of words back there," Jack said, still leaning against her. "I apologize for it. We should join the kids at the ice-cream parlor before Eric challenges Brian to any kind of banana-split-eating contest."

"I agree," Lacey said, trying to keep her voice steady. By unspoken mutual agreement, they weren't touching anymore, walking on the hard sand away from the waves. She slipped on her shoes when they reached the van, using the puddle of light around it in the parking lot to brush off as much of the stray sand as she could. Lacey's heart was still pounding so hard she thought it would jump out of her chest.

The lights in the ice-cream parlor seemed very bright, and the people quite loud. After sharing the beach with Jack, anything that involved other people probably would have struck her that way, Lacey decided. It was hard to look at him with the kids clamoring around them. She was afraid of what she might see in his face. So Lacey made small talk, wiped ice cream off Britt, and got everyone ready for the drive back.

By the time the van pulled into their driveway, Brittany was asleep, and the other three were talking softly in the back. Jack insisted on carrying Britt upstairs for Lacey and depositing her on the bed. "From here on out she's all yours," Jack said, whispering. "I know nothing about the mysteries of Mary Janes and ruffles and have absolutely no desire to learn."

The screen door closed downstairs, and Lacey could hear Brian walking across the living room. Becca, she supposed, was still outside saying good night to Eric, a situation that she couldn't allow to go on too long, Lacey knew.

Jack stopped her in the hall outside Britt's room, sliding his fingers down her arm again to capture her wrist. "I can't help myself. Your hands are beautiful. We need to do a new advertising brochure for the store. It will be mostly hand shots. You game to try modeling?"

His question startled Lacey. It was the last thing she had thought he had in mind. "Let me think about it, okay?" she said softly, aware that they were still outside Brittany's door.

"Don't think about it so long you get doubts. Think of it as another adventure." He pulled her close to him and kissed her softly; then his mouth traveled up the side of her face to plant one last kiss at her temple.

He gave her a long look, then turned and went slowly downstairs. At the door he flicked on the porch light, then opened the door loudly.

"Got to give them plenty of warning," he said dryly and walked out. Becca walked in the door a minute later, a goofy look on her face that Lacey would have said something about if she hadn't suspected that it mirrored her own. At the street, the car started up and pulled away. Lacey went upstairs to get Britt into pajamas while she was asleep, never an easy task.

For the first time in months there was no need to tell Becca to keep her music turned down while her sister slept. It was pulsing a soft, romantic beat when Lacey came out of Britt's room. She stood in front of Becca's door, wondering if they needed to talk.

The cat wound between her ankles and purred, making a plaintive sound. Lacey took her hand off the door and headed downstairs. The cat's needs were easy to satisfy. A can of food, fifteen minutes of play, and a piece of yarn would satisfy him. At this point, with the sound of the surf still pounding in her ears, Lacey knew that Becca's questions would probably be as hard to answer as her own. It would take some soul searching before she was ready to answer either.

Nine

"You want me to get a what?"

"A manicure," Jack said patiently, leaning over Lacey's desk and using one finger to gently push up her drooping glasses. "And charge it to Dalton's Jewelry. Then be very, very nice to those hands until you come in here again. We're going to start shooting the brochure tomorrow."

"I'd almost forgotten about it," Lacey admitted.

Jack looked at her as if she'd sprouted another head. "You're kidding."

"Not at all. I've got enough to do just to get the books straight." *And keep busy while you're around,* Lacey told herself silently, looking at Jack, just as tempting as ever in his red braces.

Jack patted her on the head. "I keep forgetting that you're on an entirely different wavelength," he said.

"Not always," Lacey said, wondering if it was right to admit it even as she said it and watched the flash in his eyes.

"No, not always. It would be easier if you weren't ever," Jack said with a groan. "Just go back to your number crunching, but get that manicure, okay?"

After she agreed, she watched him walk away from her. Different wavelength indeed. Before Jack came along, Lacey would have said her life was stable, predictable, a little boring, but just fine. Now it all looked terribly dreary when compared with moonlit walks on the beach and games of basketball in the driveway.

Her tightly controlled plans were crumbling, and frightening as it seemed, Lacey almost found herself wishing for another moonlit walk with Jack. She didn't know how she would really handle a life as unpredictable as hers would become if she let Jack all the way into it, but if she was sure that was what God had in mind for her, she would be more comfortable taking it on. As things stood, she struggled, a lot, and still had no clear answer.

While she struggled, though, she was getting plenty done. The books were no longer a mess, but she was starting to get uneasy about what she was finding. There were a few little oddities, but none as glaring as the checks to Kimberly Thompson. She should have come right out by now and confronted Jack with her suspicions. Still, something held her back.

The same sense made her wait for the perfect time to deliver the other bad news she had for Jack Dalton. Even if the mess with the books was somehow not his fault and he was honest, Jack didn't belong in the business he was in, exactly. Lacey suspected that deep in his heart Jack knew both the facts she wanted to confront him with and would welcome neither. How she was going to work either subject into polite conversation she had no idea, so she just kept storing them away.

Jack stuck his head into the office again before she left. "Don't forget about the shoot tomorrow. Wear something short sleeved and comfortable because we're going to keep you hopping. And please, Lacey…"

"I know—be nice to my hands."

"Call in for pizza or let Becca cook dinner or something."

"Calling in for pizza *is* her idea of cooking dinner," Lacey said, wrinkling her nose.

"And don't go home and sit at that computer terminal either. You'll chip your polish."

Lacey sighed. "But, Jack, I've been putting in so much time

here I'm getting behind for my regular tax customers. It is that time of year, you know. February is when things start heating up."

"I know, and I'm sorry, but Valentine's Day is our biggest sale, and that brochure has to be done, on top of the books. I knew this was all a mess, but I never realized it would be this complicated. I'll let you go back to your other clients soon, I promise, even if it means hiring someone else." Jack turned and went back to his workroom before Lacey could tell him how unappealing that sounded. Shrugging, she started getting her files in order to leave for the night, though how much she would be able to work on them with newly manicured nails was anybody's guess.

The manicure was a completely new experience. After an hour of soaking, creaming, and pampering, Lacey was beginning to rethink her career choice. Thanks to Jack, she was doing that a lot lately. Around him she wanted to let go and do things that were different. She didn't want to sit in a small room and explain to people year after year why their motor home wasn't a business expense simply because they put a mobile phone in it, and that no, they couldn't deduct the dog as a dependent.

Being around Jack brought out conflicting feelings in Lacey. She had no less responsibility to the children than she had had before she met Jack. Now, along with the guilt that spending time with Jack instead of the kids brought on, there were also feelings that she should take care of herself, like she was doing now. She sat examining her soft, smooth hands. How long had it been since she'd had an hour like this to devote purely to herself? Maybe it would be worth it to have someone else be the boss for a change, even if that somebody was Jack Dalton. She wouldn't have to work so hard, and she would get a few benefits. If she was honest with herself, Lacey could admit that the biggest benefit would be spending every day with Jack.

She waggled her fingers gently, reveling in the soft new shine of her nails. It was time for Cinderella to turn back into Aunt Lacey and see if the house was still standing.

It was, just barely. Music was blaring from the stereo, but not loud enough to cover the shrieking in the family room. The kids had apparently made it through dinner without any major arguments because the kitchen was basically clean, pizza box in the trash and glasses in the sink. Lacey could tell that sometime since, Britt had gotten tired of nagging her sister and gotten her own dessert. She shooed Oops off the kitchen countertop. Kitty prints through the milk splatters and cookie crumbs testified to how the cat had enjoyed Britt's efforts.

Lacey went into the family room, switched off the music, and waited the few seconds until both combatants realized they were creating the only volume in the room. "Well?"

Brian merely rolled his eyes heavenward and flopped onto the couch dramatically. Becca was more communicative. She gestured in a broad sweep. "Do you know what he did? I can't believe it."

"Tell me, so I can decide whether to believe it or not myself," Lacey said.

"I was expecting a call, and he picked up the phone. But does he give to me? Nooooo. He tells Eric that I'm in the bathroom painting my toenails silver."

"Well, you were," Brian said, trying to do a handstand on the couch cushions.

"It's not the kind of thing you tell somebody on the phone," Becca wailed, heading for him again.

Lacey separated them quickly. "No bloodshed. Both of you

retreat to your rooms and finish the homework you're about to tell me you've already done."

"Can I take the phone in there with me?" Becca asked.

"Until eight-thirty. Then it gets hung up for the night."

Becca sighed in exaggerated dimensions but left the room. Lacey sat down next to Brian on the couch. "That wasn't real cool, sport," she said as he slipped into an upright position.

"I know," he said before a grin escaped. "But it's so much fun."

"Upstairs. Move. And take a shower before bed."

"Okay. Are my black jeans clean?"

"I'll find out," Lacey said, going into the laundry room and looking around. She lifted things gingerly until she found the jeans. Great. They and the only other pants Brian would dream of wearing to school right now were both dirty. She carefully put a dark load into the washer and started it.

Going upstairs she knocked on Becca's door and stuck her head in. "Put the wash in the dryer for me when it's done, okay?"

Becca, hand over the phone, nodded. She grabbed Lacey's hand for a moment and inspected it. "Okay. Nice," she said, then resumed her conversation. "Hmm. Oh, it's only my aunt. Right…"

Lacey closed the door softly and went into Brittany's room. She picked a path through the stuffed animals and toys on the floor until she could sit on the bed beside Britt, who had changed into pajamas and was absorbed in a book.

"Want me to read to you for a while before bed?"

Britt slipped under the covers. "Sure. But not this one. This one I can read myself. Read out of the green book."

Lacey crossed to the shelves and got the book, heavy in her

hand. She sat back down on the bed and held the book in her lap. It fell open to a particular spot, as Lacey knew it would, and she read the fairy tale the book opened to.

"That was always my favorite," she said to Britt when she was done. "Your mom read to me most nights in the room we shared, and she didn't figure out for over a year that I liked that one best because it was the longest story in the book."

Britt giggled. "I like it too. And it is long."

Lacey looked at her watch. "Long enough that it's time for lights out." She kissed the little girl's cheek as she snuggled down into the bedcovers. At the door she turned out the light, making sure a small night-light was glowing, then shut the door.

In her own room she changed into an oversized sleep shirt, careful not to snag her nails on anything as she did so.

As the sleep shirt slid over her head, Lacey looked in the mirror. It was the same person staring back, and yet it wasn't.

This person, she had to admit, wasn't as thrilled with her straight hair and plain brown glasses as she had been a month ago. This person was beginning to notice that T-shirts were undoubtedly more fun than suits. This person really got a kick out of roller-skating at the rink, even with six-year-olds. This person just might be falling in love.

The thought made her shiver. Love didn't have any place in this well-ordered schedule she had mapped out for herself. Not for at least a few more years, when more of the kids were launched and gone. It was just not possible. Lacey turned away from the mirror. It was time to find something to do. But what? Most of her usual diversions from thinking about Jack, like housework and her work at the computer, were out.

She padded over to the bed and looked at the nightstand. Her current reading material other than her Bible consisted of financial magazines, updates on tax-code changes, and one book: *Sibling Warfare, or How to Keep Your Kids from Killing Each Other* the glossy cover proclaimed. She settled onto the bed. With her battling brood, anything was worth a try.

She woke up an hour later with a kink in her neck. The book had worked the way it usually did; she was out like a light by page ten. The people who wrote this book must not have had real children, Lacey decided. There were never any "conflict resolution solutions" about what to do when your ten-year-old nearly gets murdered by his sister for embarrassing her over the phone or how to handle a six-year-old's scientific experiments using cats and laundry chutes. She shrugged and put the book back on the nightstand.

Maybe she'd bring it up with Jack tomorrow. He was the only one in living memory that had gotten Brian and Becca to cooperate with each other pleasantly. Maybe it came from being a "big brother" to Eric and growing up with a kid brother. From what he said, he and Jamie had always gotten along all right. Maybe he'd have some solutions.

Even if he didn't, it would be a nice safe topic of conversation during a day spent with him. Lacey was running out of nice, safe topics of conversation around Jack. For about the thousandth time, she wished she could talk to Beth, even just for ten minutes.

She would ask her what to do about Britt's nightmares and how she had kept the kids from squabbling with each other. Beth had everything so well planned out. They'd been the perfect family—perfectly spaced, names that went together just right on their Christmas cards. Then Lacey took over, and she felt that things would never be the same again.

Of course they weren't. No two people raised children alike, she told herself. And besides, she'd had the aftermath of the auto accident to deal with, the funerals, and the grief, the counseling. But still, she'd like to talk to Beth. While she had her here, she would ask her what falling in love felt like.

Lacey was afraid she already knew the answer to that one. It felt scary and tense, like she needed to take a long walk about three times a day. And it felt nice at the same time, when it wasn't terrifying. She snapped off the light and pushed the cat off the bed. He stalked off in royal dudgeon to go find Becca or someone else who would tolerate his sleeping on their bed. Lacey drifted off to sleep listening to the rumblings of the Siamese down the hall as he attempted to open bedroom doors.

Ten

J ack looked around the office. Slowly Lacey had taken over without his ever being aware of it. There was a high-intensity lamp on the desk that dispelled the gloom in the dingy corner. And when had she painted? Maybe she'd just scrubbed the walls thoroughly before she put up the charts and the neat printed list of phone numbers. Jamie's office was a real workspace again.

She'd left the calendar the way it was. Jack knew that had to be a concession to him. Lacey thought it was macabre. For him it was simple. A part of time had stopped that night Jamie drove his car into the abutment, and it wasn't ever going to start again in this lifetime. He looked closer. The calendar hadn't been changed, but it had been dusted. That was Lacey. Precise and concerned with detail.

The drawers were full of neatly sharpened pencils and ruled paper and a portable calculator. The files kept down here were in order, and everything was wiped clean of the dust and grime that had accumulated. Jack was amazed she had stayed long enough to do all this.

Any day now, the spell was going to break. She was going to put all the little puzzles together, and he was going to have to explain everything, and then she would be gone. At least she had stayed this long. After today he would have reminders of Lacey all over, in the new brochure, in every newspaper ad they took out for a while. Perhaps it would be enough to call up her memory once she left. And Jack was certain that soon she *would* leave.

Jack wanted a cup of coffee before the photographer called

them to start shooting. He went up to the kitchen, careful to stay out of the way of the people setting up for the shoot in his living room.

When he got back downstairs, Lacey was at her desk. She looked a little out of place, just sitting there, hands in her lap. She waggled her fingers at him. "Look at this. You've created a monster. I can't even use the phone without using a pencil to push buttons."

"But you look great." She was more elegant than he imagined with pale polish and shaped nails. He took one hand and inspected it. "Perfect."

Lacey smiled at him. "You smell good. Cologne and fresh coffee. Think you could get me a cup? After all, you don't want me to ruin these perfect nails," she teased.

"Sure." Jack felt the need for some space between them anyway. He went to look for a cup.

By noon it felt like the day had been two weeks long. Jack hadn't expected that putting jewelry on Lacey for a photo shoot would affect him as much as it did.

"You really like what you create, don't you?" she said, looking up at him. She seemed as affected as he was by the close contact, though she also seemed to be trying to diffuse her own feelings.

"This is different," he told her. "Usually I see people buy things, they take them away, and I'm not involved anymore. Today I'm plenty involved." It was strange realizing just how involved he was getting by simply helping Lacey get ready for each photo shot.

When Carla, the photographer, insisted on shooting a wedding set, it was the worst. "You did want these in the brochure, didn't you?" Carla asked Jack, puzzled at his reaction.

"Well, sure," he began. "But I'd totally forgotten it was a

three-ring set." Carla had been doing his photo shoots for two years now and was very practical. She walked up to him and looked at his hands, her brow wrinkling in concentration.

"You'll do," she said finally. "Especially if we put her hand on top of yours. Roll down your sleeves and get over there."

Jack slipped the rings on Lacey first. They were a breathtaking pair that wove together, the diamond engagement band nestling into the wedding ring so that they joined. The man's ring had the same sweeping design in a broad gold band. Jack grimaced as he slipped it on.

"What's the matter?" Lacey asked.

"Too tight," he said, looking down at his hand. "But then, maybe any wedding ring would be too tight for me."

"These are beautiful, Jack," Lacey said softly. "You made them yourself, your own design."

"You can tell?" Jack was surprised.

Carla walked over and started placing their hands. Lacey's hand felt so small on top of his hand, so warm, so right. For a moment a host of goofy images played around him, all of things he had sworn would never happen to him. He could see himself cutting a wedding cake and feeding her a bite, his car in a parking lot being decorated with shaving cream and tin cans and a Just Married sign.

He glanced over at Lacey. She seemed to be fighting for composure as well. She looked down at their hands, looking at the rings. "I've seen enough of your designs now that I can recognize them. They've got a power, an individuality," Lacey said and then faltered.

"Go on," Jack urged. "Tell me more." He found it hard to concentrate on anything but her hand draped over his.

"Are we having fun yet?" Lacey asked softly, unable to keep a teasing note out of her voice.

"So it isn't as much fun as I thought," he said tersely.

Lacey looked thoughtful. "Why do you keep selling other stuff? Why not just do the custom work you're so good at? Anybody can sell gold watches, Jack."

"Are you putting down my family business?" he asked. He couldn't tell her that the answer had to do with a check made out to Kimberly Thompson, a check that suddenly seemed to be burning a hole in his shirt pocket. It wasn't Lacey's fault, but he couldn't keep the anger out of his voice. The muscles under Lacey's fingers tightened with his tension.

"Your family business? No, not at all." She looked wary and confused. Jack knew there wasn't much he could say to smooth things over.

"Well, this is the way my folks set things up. They wanted it this way, and Jamie wanted it this way. It's supposed to be a family jewelry store."

"Jack, relax your fingers. You're clenching up," Carla said. He made his fingers slacken.

"But your folks are retired from this end of the business. You're the one in charge now, Jack."

"Sure," Jack said quickly. "But I don't think I'd be any better at managing a custom jewelry store than a regular one."

Carla came to his rescue before Lacey could keep the argument going. She bustled in, changed their positions, and whisked Jack away to get another tray of jewelry to keep them on the strict shooting schedule. Pulling off the constricting gold band, it was all he could do not to cheer.

Well, she'd botched that one. The attempt to have a casual discussion about changing the nature of the business with Jack had been a failure. And Lacey didn't have another opportunity to try to make things right all afternoon. They didn't break for lunch until after two, and even then it was a quick sandwich and a cold glass of iced tea standing up, held gingerly in her still-to-be-pampered fingers.

Leona clucked over her as she ate. "You need to sit down and do that," she said, trying to find Lacey a chair.

"Can't. We've got to get the last of the brochure shot, and I know what this is costing Jack," Lacey said between bites.

"It is a lot," Leona agreed. "If only he'd let me try my hand at the layout anyway."

"Oh?"

Leona smiled. "I finished two years of art school about a thousand years ago, back before I married Harve and had kids. Then we moved down here, and I started working for the Daltons. I'd love to try my hand at art projects again. I've got so many ideas. Now if Jackson there could only forget I'm the old lady who helped him tie his bow tie for the prom and look at me like a promising graphic artist…"

Lacey could hear the wistful, hopeful note in her voice. "Jackson, huh? Maybe we can work something out yet," she said. "We'll go to lunch tomorrow and plot."

Then Carla was ready again, and Lacey didn't come up for air until the photographer packed up and left and they all sat around the apartment in the rubble of rearranged furniture following the shooting of the final pictures.

Jack popped open a soda and sprawled on the couch. "What do you say to me taking you two ladies out to dinner at six after we close the shop?"

"Sounds good to me," Lacey murmured, trying to massage a kink out of her calf.

"Sorry," Leona said, shaking her head. "Harve already topped your offer. He knew I was having a rough day, and he's cooking. I can't miss that."

"Okay. Looks like it's just you and me, then." Jack turned to Lacey. "How about the Bubble Room?"

Lacey grimaced, picturing the noisy happy hour in the popular restaurant. "Ugh. How about coming home with me and ordering pizza in? We can feed the kids, check homework, and I can take off these shoes."

"Ah, the essence of romance," Jack quipped. "Actually, it sounds pretty good. Make mine extra pepperoni."

Lacey went downstairs to her desk to make her phone calls. The one to the local pizza delivery was quick. The one home, to let them know what was going on, wasn't. It should have been a quick thing, but it wasn't. There were arguments to break up, decisions to be made on who was allowed to go where for how long before she got home, and advice on how to keep Oops from dancing on the kitchen countertop. Lacey was vaguely aware of the bell's ringing in the front and Jack's drifting through.

While Becca went on, Lacey idly straightened the contents of her desk. The check register was open again. Jack had written a check for Carla. She was pleased that he was getting much better about dating the stubs and providing lots of information. Her constant harping was getting somewhere.

Getting ready to close the register, she felt a cold shock go through her. The check before Carla's was another to Kimberly Thompson. Maybe her kitchen table over pizza was the place to discuss this. If she continued to work here, she had to know what was going on with this mystery woman.

True, she could be an innocent consultant or some sort of

supplier with a very regular bill, but Lacey didn't think so. Some sense told her that there were problems here that she needed to discuss with Jack.

Becca's tone of voice told Lacey her mind had been wandering. "I said, I need to call Eric, okay?"

"Okay, fine," Lacey said, hanging up. Jack still hadn't come back. She went through to the front of the shop. He wasn't there, but Lacey could see a flash of red suspenders down the block.

She opened the door of the shop and started down the pavement to catch up with him and tell him she was ready to go.

She stopped abruptly a few feet from the door. Just yards away, a very young woman stood on the sidewalk talking to Jack. But neither could see Lacey unless they broke their conversation, which they looked unlikely to do.

"Never—do you hear me, Kimberly?—never walk in that front door again looking for money. At least come to the back of the store, as we agreed, or I'll mail the check."

Lacey could hear the young woman's calm, reasonable answer to Jack's tirade. "There was no answer at the back, and I need the check today. The rent's due, and Kenton needs shoes."

The blond little boy hanging on her blue-jeans leg heard his name. "Are we going to the place with balloons, Mama? Can we go now?"

Lacey was getting dizzy. She knew it was time to go back into the shop and pretend she hadn't seen or heard any of this.

"Kenton, get back in the car. Now." The woman's voice was brittle.

"Okay, Mama. Bye, Daddy Jack," the little voice piped up.

Both of the adults reacted as if the child had picked up a coral snake. "Kenton!" his mother snapped.

"Did you teach him that?" Jack said in a harsh tone Lacey had never heard before. "Because if you did, you can unteach him right now, understand?"

"Don't worry, Jack. It won't happen again."

Daddy Jack. Lacey's head swam, and she bolted back into the store. Could this really be the reason Jack was paying a strange woman every month? She sat down at her desk, hands shaking. Lacey felt so numb she couldn't even form words for prayer. There was only the same phrase running through her mind over and over again. *Help me, Father. I can't handle this one alone. Help me.* Lacey saw her own hand reach out and punch in the numbers for her home phone with shaking fingers. She instructed Becca to order pizza and go ahead and eat without them. "Jack and I will be there eventually. I don't know quite when," she told her. In truth she wasn't sure Jack would ever be coming home with her again, but this was no time to explain to Becca. She hung up as the bell over the front door rang. Jack was back in the shop.

She was still feeling the effects of a day spent in close proximity to Jack and of that bang-up ending. He had been so close to her all day that Lacey suspected when she put her head on the pillow tonight, his scent, crisp and compelling, would follow her there.

"So, want to go get ice cream to take home with the pizza?" Jack asked.

"No. I'm not going anywhere tonight except home. I have to catch up on laundry and client files," Lacey said forcefully.

"Lacey, anything has got to sound better than that," Jack said. "How about dancing? Ever since I saw you on skates I've wondered if you move that well without wheels on your feet."

"Truly, I mean no," Lacey said, still feeling so hurt and angry that she didn't know how to tell Jack.

He sensed her discomfort and came over to her desk. "What's the matter?" Jack put his hand on hers, and it took all her concentration not to draw away.

Lacey took a deep breath. "After I called home, I came out to tell you I was ready. But you were busy."

Jack's face looked grim. For a moment he didn't speak. "That was Kimberly Thompson," he finally said. "You've seen the checks, I gather."

Lacey shook off his hand still covering hers and looked up into his hazel eyes. "Yes, and now I want to know the story to go along with them."

Jack inhaled, then let out the air in a long sigh as he sat down in his own office chair nearby. "Get comfortable. I'm not sure I understand all of it myself."

"Oh? What's there to understand? I think even Brian would know the facts of life that led to this one," Lacey snapped.

Jack looked up, eyes wide. "Whoa. You are making some assumptions here that don't match up with reality, Lacey."

"That little boy called you Daddy," Lacey said simply.

"No, he didn't. He called me Daddy Jack. Kimberly didn't teach him to say that. He's just confused. His daddy's gone, so now he's looking for another. Lacey, he's Jamie's son."

The room was warm, and Lacey felt her head swimming. "Jamie's," she said slowly as she looked back at Jack. "You still have plenty of talking to do. Start."

Jack talked for most of an hour. Lacey ached for him by the time he was done telling her about finding out about Jamie's other life, his girlfriend, and his new nephew.

"He would never have told me at all, I don't think, if I hadn't started checking on the supplies account. I just wanted to make sure he was buying all the gold he claimed to be because we always seemed to be short. Do you know I only met her twice before Jamie died? And I never saw Kenton until two weeks after Jamie's funeral."

He looked drained, slumped in his chair. There was so much more Lacey needed to know, even as his accountant. As his friend she wanted to gather him in her arms and tell him how she wanted to make all the hurt mirrored in those hazel eyes go away. Instead of doing either she simply took his hand for a minute and let him sit in silence.

"Otherwise things have just been fun and games lately," he said, sounding shaky.

"Now, Jack..." Lacey began, then trailed off. She didn't know quite how to voice her concern yet.

He took a sip of his tea and then another as he sat looking at her, his brow wrinkling a little. "I forgot. You and I have a different opinion of what fun and games are."

"I guess we do," Lacey said slowly. "For you, life seems to be mostly something to be enjoyed, with a little work thrown in because you have to once in a while."

"And for you it's the other way around," Jack said, slipping his hand away. "Only you don't give yourself much pleasure between times, just more work."

"Not really. I do plenty of things for myself," Lacey countered.

"Name three," Jack said, the sparkle in his eyes flashing golden.

"Well, there's my skating. And my reading, except I haven't read much lately. And—" Lacey faltered a bit. She couldn't stand the smug look on Jack's face. "There's working for you. Now that's been a challenge."

"A challenge is not the same as fun," Jack argued.

"Sometimes it is. I've enjoyed untangling your books. Honestly, Jack."

He shook his head in disbelief. "You can really sit here and tell me you enjoy leaning over these accounts all day trying to make sense of them—"

"I really can," Lacey said, deciding to plunge in with both feet. "And that's why you need to get someone on a full-time basis who enjoys it too. You've got a good business there, Jack, and I'd hate to see it go to ruin."

"The right kind of people for a job like that don't just come out of the air, Lacey. I've only known two in my life—you and Jamie. And we all know how good my judgment was with him." He looked defeated. "How do I find the right person again and convince them to work for me?"

"I'm sure you could find a way," Lacey said, not willing to give in.

"Sure. I'm supposed to corner some financial wizard and say, 'Excuse me, you look like just the person to come manage my jewelry store. It's not real profitable because my brother was dipping into the accounts to support a family nobody knew he had, and he screwed up our profits, but I'm sure you won't mind that.' And they're going to jump at the chance to work for Jack Dalton. Yeah, I can really see that one."

Lacey sat, both palms flat on the desk. She could feel the little dents in the metal. "You knew about that part too?"

"Lacey, even I am not that dense when it comes to accounting. I knew. Not in time to do anything about it, but I've at least suspected. I guess that's why I hired you in the first place, just to find out how bad it really was." Jack looked so defeated for a moment that Lacey couldn't get as indignant as she felt.

"So when were you intending to tell me?"

"When I worked up the courage," Jack said softly. "Is this a confusing conversation for you, too?"

"Very." Lacey's voice sounded brittle even to her. "Especially when I was on the brink of telling you that if you wanted the job filled, I was a candidate."

Jack reached over and clasped her arm. "This is like an answer to prayer. Only I've stopped praying."

"Then it's definitely time to start again, Jack," she informed him. "It's definitely time to start."

Eleven

Jack's grip on her arm slowly loosened. "Do you really mean what you said?"

"About prayer? I wouldn't have it any other way," Lacey told him.

"I know that. What about working for me?"

"I said I was thinking of telling you I'd be a candidate for the job. It looks like a good one. Interesting, challenging, something different. Or at least it did until this afternoon."

"And how do you feel now?"

"Like I'd have to be crazy to say I'm still interested." Jack's face was tense, as he almost willed her to answer. "But then, my kids all say I'm crazy anyway. And God has led me into some pretty crazy things before, so maybe I'll just have to trust him on this one."

Jack leaned back in his chair. "You're braver than I am, Lacey. After what I've told you tonight, are you telling me you'd like to be my business manager?"

"Especially after this," Lacey said, losing her grin. "If you hadn't told me, I wouldn't be interested. Now that I know at least this much, I feel better about working for you."

Jack shook his head, his dark brows knitting together. "Then I guess it pays to tell the truth. You really want to try this?"

Lacey nodded. "I'd like to try the job on for size. It would be a few weeks before I could do it full-time exclusively. It's almost tax season, and I've got quite a few repeat clients. To say they'll not be happy if I leave them at this time of year is an understatement. Plus I'd like to figure out how comfortable I am with the whole situation."

"Take all the time you like," Jack said, breaking into a grin. "I'd be very happy to have you even half-time, Lacey."

"We need to talk more before I make a final decision, Jack. I need to know more about you, and Jamie, and a few other things before you hire me."

"I understand that, but this isn't the time or place," Jack said. "I know it is terribly ungentlemanly of me to notice, but you look beat. I think we need to call it a night."

Lacey couldn't argue. "Please."

Jack stood up. "And I think I'll take a rain check on going to your house for pizza. I seem to have lost my appetite. We aren't exactly calm, casual conversationalists, are we? I promise, sometime I'll make all of this up to you."

His expression showed her that Jack really believed what he was saying. So far, being around Jack was like being in a high windstorm, and Lacey couldn't imagine that with him, things would ever calm down for long.

"Let me walk you to your car," he told her. "I have something to show you."

The air outside was cool and teased her hair off her hot face. Jack's arm around her as they walked out of the store felt very good, especially when Lacey realized just how tired she was.

Jack locked up behind them and pocketed the keys, then walked with her to the parking lot.

When they reached her car, he leaned over and kissed her sweetly. Slowly he ended the kiss and pulled away, still leaning with one hand against her car. With the other hand he reached into his pants pocket and pulled out a shiny black-satin box. It was small and gave Lacey a sinking feeling deep inside.

"What are you doing?" she asked softly, trying not to show her panic at what was going to be a gift she couldn't accept.

"I saw you admiring this during the photo shoot today." He opened the box to show a small filigreed ring with a pale green stone. "I just wanted to give it to you. My way of saying thank you for a long day of hard work."

"And nothing else?"

Jack looked puzzled. "Nothing else. It's not a bribe to get you to take the job full-time or anything. Just a way of showing my appreciation for a job well done."

Lacey looked down at the ring. It gleamed against the satin of the box, glowing in the pale evening light. Of course there was nothing else. Jack made jewelry for a living, and he would attach no sentimentality to a hunk of gold and stones.

"I shouldn't take this, even as this kind of gift, but I will," Lacey said. She couldn't repress her shiver of delight when Jack slipped it onto her right ring finger.

"Looks nice," he said, holding her hand out to examine the ring. "Even the perfect size."

"It's beautiful, like all of your work," she said.

Jack drew her close to him again. His hug was tight and quick. "Thank you so much for being here tonight, for hearing me out."

"I wouldn't have it any other way," Lacey told him. She pulled away reluctantly. "I have to go, Jack. It's another early morning tomorrow."

"Tomorrow's Saturday," Jack protested as she pulled away.

"Yup, Saturday. That means six loads of laundry, grocery shopping, making sure the bathrooms are clean, one soccer practice, one dance-recital costume fitting, and one session at the rink."

"How do you do it, Lacey? Don't you ever want to just

chuck everything and vamoose to a desert island?"

Lacey knew her expression was hard. "Of course. But I don't have that choice. These are children, as in real people. They're my responsibility for keeps."

"Okay." Jack's hands were held palm up in protest. "I didn't mean to doubt your commitment. It's just that I don't know if I could ever do that."

Lacey tried to brush it off casually, even though she felt like taking his broad shoulders and shaking him. "Well, I can, and I do. But I do it better with eight hours' sleep."

"Sleep well, then," Jack said. There was frustration in the hard edges of his voice as he dropped one last soft kiss on her nose before he drew away. "And be careful driving home."

"I will," Lacey promised. Jack stood and watched as she got into the car and started the ignition, only moving when she had her lights on, the engine purring, and was ready to pull out of the lot.

The drive home was a bit blurry. Lacey was so tired and so overwhelmed by her feelings that she felt as though she were on automatic pilot.

At home she parked and went in the front door, foot instinctively sticking out to keep the cat from escaping outside.

Lacey looked around. The living room seemed undisturbed except for the cat perched on the back of the couch. He padded across the floor, giving his unearthly guttural call to convince her to give him another meal.

"Can opened in one minute," she said, heading toward the kitchen. "You can admire my present while you eat." She caught the moonlight streaming in a side window as she walked to the kitchen. "Or you can admire the tuna while I admire the ring." She sat in the kitchen and they did just that.

There was a flash of silver-white deep in the pale green

stone when Lacey moved her hand in the light. It flowed like a vein through the ring, and she thought of Jack. Somewhere in him there was a vein like this, liquid and flashing, touched by the Spirit, that he hid from her most of the time. But she sensed that it was there under the surface. Whether or not he wanted it that way, she brought it to light. The ring picked up a particle of light from the fixture, fractured it, and threw a glistening pattern across the ceiling. Lacey sat on a stool, watching it and listening while Oops muttered love songs to his rapidly disappearing dinner.

Saturday was every bit as hectic as Lacey thought it was going to be. Worse, because soccer practice ended late, the costume fitting took twice as long as she expected, and no one told her they were out of flour until she unloaded the groceries, put them away, and started to fix dinner.

Of course, once she yelled up the stairs that she was going back to the grocery store, everybody had a last request. It took her another forty-five minutes to gather two more bags of groceries, pay for them, shove them into the van, and come back.

Plenty had happened at home during that time. Lacey could tell by the flung-open windows and Jack's car in the driveway.

"Perhaps someone would like to explain all of this to me," Lacey said as she kicked open the door, a bag of groceries on each arm. The house smelled peculiar, and there were voices in the kitchen.

"Hi," Jack said, sounding a little sheepish. "I'm glad you're home."

"So am I. Just drop in to say hello?"

"Well, not exactly," Jack said. "I came over to keep Brittany company and to explain to her why we don't tell people on the telephone that we're home alone."

"Britt!" Lacey's voice stopped her from slinking out the back door. "Why were you home alone, and what have I told you about that, anyway?"

"I was home alone because Becca got picked up to go baby-sit for the Hendersons and Brian finished his shower and said he could too go over to Scott's to shoot baskets because you hadn't told him he couldn't, and then Jack called." Britt stopped for breath, satisfied that she'd explained everything.

Lacey bent down to her level, putting an arm around her as she knelt. "Okay, but even if you are home alone, what do you tell people on the phone? Remember?"

"Sure. That you're in the shower or something and can't come to the phone. But it was only Jack."

Lacey tried not to shake her head in despair. "No matter who's on the other end of the line, don't say you're home alone, okay? And next time—" She stopped herself. "There won't be a next time after I skin both your brother and your sister."

Britt slipped outside, and Lacey started pulling groceries out of sacks. "They all know better than that," she said to Jack, trying to control her frustration. She set the bag of flour down so hard it raised a small cloud of white dust.

Jack was beside her with a dish towel. "I expect they do. I was concerned when Brittany was so free about telling me she was home all alone and didn't know where anybody else was or when they'd be back. Especially when she told me her great adventure."

"Adventure?"

"Well, it seems that she forgot to take the wrapper off the toaster pastry before she zapped her snack."

Lacey looked toward the microwave. "Incinerated another one, huh?"

"That's about the size of it." Jack grimaced. "I had visions of calling the fire department. Of course, once I'd zoomed over here and realized that Brian was across the street and you were a few blocks away getting groceries, I felt like a fool."

"Join the club. Kids will do that to you."

"Every time." There was a bitterness there that Lacey hadn't expected. It made her wonder just how much involvement Jack had with Kimberly.

She went to the refrigerator and poured them each a glass of tea, then led Jack to the table. His eyes questioned her, but he sat.

"Last night might not have been the time or place, but this is as good as any, Jack Dalton. I want to know more about your brother and your relationship with him before I go to work for you."

"And if I refuse to tell you?"

If he thought he could force her hand, Jack had another thing coming. He had the same defiant tilt to his head that Lacey often saw in her teenagers. It didn't look any better on him. "If you refuse, I can choose to keep being a tax accountant, working for myself. It's boring sometimes, but it's real safe."

Jack sighed and looked down into his glass of tea, clinking ice cubes against the side of the glass. Finally he spoke. "Jamie was an alcoholic. I guess when I think back on it, he probably had been in trouble for years."

Somehow this wasn't the answer she expected. "Wasn't he younger than you?"

"Eighteen months. Age didn't have anything to do with it. When we were in high school, Jamie was the jock. Football, baseball, you name it, he always had a place on the team. I thought at the time that the partying was just because of the

111

crowd he ran with. Later I decided that he ran with that crowd to cover the amount he was drinking."

"In high school?"

Jack nodded, a vacancy to his stare as one hand polished the tabletop absentmindedly. His shoulders were tight, hunched protectively around his pain. It was almost an automatic gesture that made Lacey stand behind him, gently massaging his shoulders as he talked. He didn't pull away, and slowly the tightness that felt like stretched wire eased from the taut muscles.

"I always covered for him. Our folks were older when they had the two of us, and I just figured they couldn't handle what Jamie was doing. So I was the one that got him home, got him to bed, got him up the next day. By the time he went to college at Gainesville, I figured he'd learned to handle things himself, that he'd grown out of the habit."

"And had he?"

"He'd learned to conceal it better," Jack said, leaning back into Lacey. His head was heavy against her midsection, and she wanted to pull him back, embrace him, and make the pain go away. But she knew that no amount of hugging could do that, and she breathed a silent prayer for him while he continued. "By the time we'd been in business together a few years I found out what else he learned to conceal. After he died, I discovered he'd been borrowing money over and above his salary to finance a few private debts."

"How much was he drinking?"

"It wasn't just for that. You see, drinking gave Jamie self-confidence. When he had enough to drink, he'd go out to the jai-alai fronton or the greyhound track or wherever else he felt lucky. He had a whole life that no one else knew about."

"Oh?" Lacey knew what was coming, but she let Jack tell it.

He went on. "He met the lovely Kimberly and set up house-keeping with her in Sanford without telling anyone. When I'd go over to the apartment, he'd be the only one in it." Jack sighed, looking out the window for a minute.

"Unfortunately, drinking may have boosted his self-confidence, but it didn't really do anything for his luck. That remained pretty lousy all the time. Maybe it's a family trait." Jack looked down again, and Lacey could feel the pain inside him. She moved to kneel in front of him.

Instead he pulled her onto his lap while he enveloped her and she him in an embrace she hoped would banish some of the demons she had raised by asking him about Jamie. "I'm sorry," she murmured into his hair.

"It's okay. You asked. I thought I could answer without getting upset. I was wrong." Any further words were lost as she pulled him close, much as she would Brittany in one of her terrors.

Even though she wanted to comfort Jack the way she did the kids, it was the last thing she expected when his breath on her neck changed to a chuckle.

Her questioning look brought a quick grin from Jack, lopsided, but gaining ground. "You smell like flour. And you're all white."

Lacey dusted the powder off of her cheeks, easing out of his arms. "I guess when I put the bag on the counter..." Looking at his eyes, deep green and bronze, she couldn't find any more words until he reached up and slipped her glasses back up her nose. "Want to stay for dinner while you're here? I know there's enough round steak, and I can always stretch mashed potatoes."

"I'd love to." Jack reached over and traced a line down her chin. The contact made her shiver, and he smiled again. "You missed a spot. The flour."

"Oh." Lacey didn't know what else to say. She busied herself getting meat out of the refrigerator to try to hide her discomfort.

"We're not done talking yet, Jack," she warned him. "But I have to get dinner on, and I'm afraid carrying on this conversation while I do so will mean I take off one of my fingers instead of peeling potatoes. I want to talk about this more. And pray about it with you."

Jack looked startled. "If you say so. Think the kids will give us some time after dinner?"

"If we steal it, perhaps," Lacey told him. "This is too important to let it slip away."

"I agree," he said solemnly, standing and coming around the kitchen counter. "Now how about if I peel potatoes while you deal with the meat. Suddenly I'm as hungry as Brian."

"That is probably impossible," Lacey told him, reaching for the bag of potatoes. "We'll have to see."

Twelve

They both tried to slip into a semblance of normal conversation. "So how did the rest of the day go?" Jack asked, pulling up a stool and sitting down to watch.

She kept him busy making a salad while he sat listening to her recital of the hectic day. Lacey noticed that he nibbled little bits of vegetables while he peeled, chopped, and prepared everything. It was nice having someone to tell her problems to, even when they were minor. Jack seemed content to simply listen quietly as he made the salad.

She finished all the details at about the time she put the last of the steak into the pan. "What about your practice this afternoon at the rink?" Jack looked at her when she didn't respond. "You did go, didn't you?"

"Yeah, I went," Lacey said, turning the first pieces of meat and watching them sizzle.

"What's the matter? Fall on your nose or something?"

"No, but I'm about to," Lacey said. "The advanced class is going to have a program in a couple weeks."

"And?"

"And they actually want me to be part of the program."

"So what? You upset because you don't have anybody to sign your permission slip?"

"Oh, Jack, be real. An old lady like me out there with all those kids? Get serious."

"I am serious." Jack put down the salad fixings and advanced toward her. "And you, Lacey, are not an old lady. You happen to be younger than I am. I know that for a fact via the teenage grapevine."

"Well, I'm older than anybody else in the class by a decade," Lacey countered. "That makes me feel ancient."

"You don't look it. And skating in a program like that definitely counts as seeking adventure, doesn't it?"

Lacey went back to cooking before she burned dinner. "That it definitely does."

"Does that mean you'll skate in the program? We'll all come cheer."

"You're on," Lacey said, unable to resist the smile that bubbled up from somewhere deep inside. "But no pictures."

"Perfectionist," Jack teased as he released her.

"You bet. Call the kids in for dinner," Lacey said, deftly flipping the meat onto a platter. Watching Jack walk to the doorway she had to suppress a giggle. She was a perfectionist, no denying it. And his retreating form in pale washed jeans definitely fit her standards of perfection. Watching him, the giggle escaped.

The next two weeks made Jack doubt his sanity each and every day. He had to have been crazy to tell Lacey he wanted her to work for him. Every day she bloomed a little more, like a rose. And every day he got closer to going insane.

The Monday after the photo shoot, she'd come back in to work, carrying a huge canvas tote bag full of office things and settled into the spot he couldn't think of as Jamie's anymore. It was undeniably Lacey's now, with her blotter, her desk accessories, the scent of her cologne rising each time he passed the desk. Jack found it hard just to pass the desk without reaching out and touching her.

Wednesday when she came in from lunch, Jack looked up to see a new woman. "You cut your hair," was all he could manage.

The look on her face wasn't at all what he'd expected. "You noticed right away."

"It's hard not to." The swing of chin-length bounce that replaced the longer, straighter cut gave new definition to her face, made Lacey seem to glow. "I like it."

"Good. When you said that right away I wasn't sure," she said, coming closer to where he was working on a set of earrings, perched on a high stool above the counter. The new lift and sheen to her hair made Jack want to bury his face in it.

The next week it was the new glasses. Fire-engine-red frames, smaller and rounder than the tortoiseshell numbers she'd traded in. Even Leona whistled when Lacey pivoted for approval. "Those are great, honey. You look more like a model every day."

Jack had to agree. Lacey was reshaping herself into a different image, and he wondered how much of that was due to him. She was too independent to want much approval from him, but if she was changing with him in mind, she was doing a great job.

"I like the suit, too," he said, standing close enough to smell the scent of violets in her perfume. The suit was black-and-white houndstooth with a short black skirt. "Becca approves, I bet."

Lacey looked troubled. "Is it too much? I did take her along to pick it out."

"It's great. But I bet it won't be in your closet a week before she borrows it."

Her grin was part grimace. "I know. I'm threatening to padlock the closet. After what she did to my favorite sweater, she's not coming near this suit."

Now, on Saturday night, standing in the near dark of the

roller rink, Jack watched Lacey limber up for her performance.

"How do you like that outfit?" Becca whispered beside him. He was afraid to tell her how much he liked it. Lacey in sleek black leggings and a long T-shirt knit tunic made his throat go dry.

Right now, she looked a little nervous. Jack motioned to Becca to catch her eye. "I'm going over there for a while."

Becca smiled. "Good. She could probably use the moral support. We'll keep an eye on the kids."

Jack suppressed his laughter. Like she and Eric weren't part of the kids. He let her have her fantasy and walked over to where Lacey stood, warming up. "You look like a lady who could use a hug," Jack said, coming up behind her.

"You are right," she said. She glided over to him, and he marveled at how their bodies fit together with the extra height the roller skates gave her. Jack folded his arms around her and gave her an embrace. He hoped it settled her down because that sure wasn't what it was doing for him.

She looked up at him and smiled. "How about a quick prayer while we're here?"

"Together?" Jack's voice sounded high even to himself.

"Together. Aloud."

"Quietly."

"Oh, all right," she said, taking his hands from her shoulders. "Heavenly Father, I am really, really nervous. Help me to remember that you're with me, even on wheels."

"Yes, Lord. Stay with us. Stay with us both," was all Jack could say. It seemed enough to Lacey.

"Amen." She squeezed his hands and broke away. Her smile was radiant. "Thanks."

"Wow. So much for nervous," Jack said.

Lacey shot him another brilliant smile. "Spring fever, I

guess. Even though the weather never does anything that looks like spring down here."

"What do you mean? Everything's bright green, and I saw four people in shorts today."

Lacey wrinkled her nose at him. "That's what I mean. Spring is forsythia and daffodils and Easter hats and all those things, not shorts in February. I'll never quite get used to it."

"Yeah, well, Chicago had a foot of snow last week. Want to get used to that again?"

Lacey shuddered. "Not in a million years."

She looked at the skaters coming off the rink. "My turn. Wish me luck."

Jack reached out and squeezed her hand as she went off. "Go for it, Lacey. We'll be watching."

"Yeah, the oldest living roller skater in Seminole County."

He winked at her and watched Lacey shiver. She did it every time, and it delighted him. Lacey smiled a wavery smile and skated off. Her shoulders were back, and she looked confident, more confident than she felt, Jack knew. Still, watching her glide and stride across the rink was like magic.

She really did well under the lights, keeping up with the teenagers in the fast-paced routine. Jack decided that this was what he liked best about Lacey. She could be all business in the office and mean every word of her hard-driving financial demands for his cleaning up the business. But when she threw herself into something, it was with the verve she was showing out there on the rink.

It made him wish once again for what he knew she had. For a faith that truly let go and let God be God, leading her along. In his world, he couldn't see it happening. Could he really sacrifice that much, that thoroughly? After Jamie's death, he had thought he had tried. Obviously it hadn't been enough because he still felt a distance from the Lord that Lacey never seemed to have. He kept watching her, the yearning in his heart causing a bittersweet ache.

To Lacey, the lights on the rink were hot, but not hot enough to keep a cool sweat from trickling down her back while she skated. The routine went well, and it was exhilarating to be turning and bouncing with the girls. It was even more exhilarating to be done, skating off the oval to let someone else take the spotlight.

Brittany was the first one to reach her in a tremendous hug "You did great! I liked it all," she said, squeezing Lacey hard.

"I'll second that motion," Jack said, coming up behind them and kissing her lightly on the neck. "Are you glad you did it?"

Lacey nodded, passing a hand over her forehead. "And even gladder that it's over, at least this first time."

Brian laughed. "Kind of like a math test, huh?"

"Sort of." She saw a look that passed between Jack and Britt. "What are you two thinking?"

"Banana split."

"I beg your pardon?" She laughed, brushing her hair away from her face.

"We're trying to figure out if we can talk you into going for ice cream. Brittany says she likes vanilla the best."

"That's Brittany. I don't know any of this crew that would turn down ice cream, though." True to form, none of them did. Becca and Eric sat at their own table, but they went.

Brittany got her vanilla, of course. Plain. Two scoops.

Lacey ruffled her hair. "Are you ever going to get anything else?"

"Nope," Britt said before she dug into her ice cream. Lacey

had successfully predicted what each child would get.

"What did I tell you?" she said, trying not to sound smug. Then she saw his expression. He looked somehow bereft as he looked down at his banana split. "What's the matter?"

"You could predict down to the nuts and sprinkles what these guys were going to eat. Even Eric, and you've only known him for a matter of weeks," Jack said. "I just realized I don't even know if Kenton likes ice cream."

Lacey put a hand on his arm. "Maybe it's time to find out."

"Maybe it is," he said, starting to spoon up some ice cream. She started paying attention to her raspberry ice. The children wolfed down their ice cream as usual, then started talking to Jack a mile a minute.

Before they knew it, Becca and Eric were standing at their table. "Mind if we walk home?" Becca asked.

Lacey looked at Jack, who shrugged. "It's okay by me."

"I guess so," Lacey said. "Turn on the lights when you get home if you beat us there."

"We will," Eric said. "We're fast walkers." They disappeared hand in hand. Sitting in the easy camaraderie of the ice-cream parlor on Saturday night, the children talked a lot. Brittany dominated the conversation just by sheer bulk, but everyone got a turn. Lacey discovered that Jack liked computer games almost as well as Brian.

After a few minutes, everyone had finished but Jack, and he was mostly pushing a cherry around in the bottom of his dish. "Go ahead," he said, watching Brian eye the fruit. "Never did like those myself anyway. Now, tell me more about this knight thing. Can you use all the weapons, or is it just some dumb word simulation?"

"No, you can use all of them. Jousting is the best," Brian said. Lacey rose to throw away all the sticky used napkins, and by the time she got back to the table, both of them looked up at her hopefully.

"Come on," she finally said. "Let's just go home, and you guys can play a round while I put Britt to bed."

"I thought you'd never ask," Jack said, a grin on his face that mirrored Brian's. They made the quick drive home, where they found the teenagers talking on the screen porch.

Lacey let them be while she got Britt's hair washed and dried and made sure she slipped into her pajamas. After that the child zipped down the hall and into the office annex to tell Jack good night. "Next time I'll play something with you, okay Britt?" Lacey could hear Jack through the open door.

"You'll regret it, man," Brian cautioned. "She likes Barbies."

"I like other things too," Britt countered.

"Yeah, like dressing Oops up in baby clothes. That's why he was up on the roof last time."

"Oops."

With that trademark statement, Brittany came back to Lacey, who managed to stifle the laughter that threatened to erupt. So that was why there had been shreds of pink ribbons on Britt's floor. Who said ignorance was bliss, anyway?

She put Brittany to bed, then turned out the light and pulled the door halfway shut. In the darkened room, the night-light blinked on, and Lacey heard the little girl sigh and settle into the covers.

At the other end of the hall, pandemonium broke loose.

"Hey, you two, pipe down," Lacey said in a loud whisper, heading for the door.

"Sorry. But I just got crowned king of England," Brian said, beaming.

"You won? That's great."

"It was Jack," Brian said, flinging an arm around him. "He

really knows how to use a catapult."

"Among other things," Lacey murmured. "Now how about getting a shower and heading for bed?"

For once Brian didn't argue. She could see him walking down the hall as if a royal diadem were perched on his head. "King Brian the first," she said softly, conscious of Jack behind her. She turned to him. "Want a cup of coffee or something? We can retreat downstairs and be grown-ups if you want."

"That's kind of a mixed blessing," Jack said with a lopsided grin. "I was enjoying watching him being crowned king of England myself."

In a few minutes they were settled on the family-room couch with mugs of coffee, something soft playing on the stereo. The cat stretched out on one arm of the sofa, watching them lazily.

"You're sore," Jack said as he watched Lacey slide gingerly onto the couch.

"A little, I guess. I've been practicing a lot for the show."

Jack put his hands on her shoulders and gently but firmly rotated her until she was facing away from him. He dug into her protesting muscles with experienced hands. The cat started purring, and Lacey said, "I know just how you feel."

Jack laughed. "That must mean I'm doing my job right."

It seemed perfect, the smoky music blending with the feel of Jack's rubbing her back. Lacey wanted to lean back against him far enough that he could see her eyes, see the love in them that she didn't think she could voice yet but that she knew shone there unbidden. As she moved, there was an unearthly scream overhead, and Jack sat up straight.

"What on earth?" he exclaimed at the high, keening wail. It was loud enough that not only did Jack leap up off the couch but Eric rushed in from the sun porch, pursued by Becca.

Lacey didn't have time to worry about that now. "You two stay down here. Becca, explain," she told her, heading for Jack. He was bolting up the stairs, Lacey behind him, before she had a chance to try to explain the noise.

Thirteen

Britt was sitting straight up in bed, plucking at the covers. Her eyes were open, but Lacey knew from experience that what she saw was not of this world. "They're there—it's on fire—they're there!" she said in a high, terror-stricken voice.

Lacey turned on a lamp in the corner so that a soft glow filled the room and then went and scooped Britt into her lap. "It's okay, Britt, we're here. It's all right. You're having a bad dream."

Jack stood near the bed, looking panicky. This was clearly not something he had experienced before. "Night terrors," Lacey said softly. "I'll explain later. For now just get me a cool, damp washcloth, okay?"

He swallowed hard and nodded, already on his way out of the room. When he came back, he knelt by the bed, a frightened look on his face that made him look more boyish than ever. "She really will be okay in a little while," Lacey said in a low voice. She rubbed the washcloth over Britt's forehead, moving the damp hair away from her face and soothing her. Already the flush was beginning to leave her skin, and she was almost quiet. Once in a while Britt muttered something, but Lacey held her and rocked her and spoke softly to her.

She did what she always did, rocking Britt like a much smaller child and slowly singing "Jesus Loves Me" very quietly, over and over.

Soon an arm had crept around Lacey's neck, and she could feel Britt's small fingers relaxing slowly. In a minute Britt shuddered, sighed, and quieted. When her breathing became regular,

Lacey handed Jack the washcloth and motioned for him to turn off the lamp. He turned it off and came back to sit beside the bed on the floor again.

His face was tense, and a muscle in his cheek twitched a little. Lacey knew there would be plenty of questions when they got downstairs. But for now there was stillness as they both sat in the darkened room and listened to Britt's soft, sweet breathing.

When Lacey was sure Britt had calmed completely and was sleeping peacefully, she slipped her back into the bed and tucked her in, nestling her favorite stuffed bear in with her. Britt hardly stirred.

After a few minutes, Lacey stepped from the room, expecting Jack to follow, but when she turned, he wasn't there. Going back to the door of Britt's room, she saw him. He stood silently for a moment, stroking Brittany's damp blond hair, then turned and followed Lacey.

Jack was quiet until they sat back down on the couch again. Then he let out a slow, ragged breath. "You want to tell me what I just saw? It looked like the junior version of the d.t.'s or something."

"That's a night terror. A very vivid dream or nightmare in which a child doesn't wake but has the same, recurring bad dream or vision."

"You sound like an expert."

Lacey gave a shaky laugh. "Not because I want to be, believe me. The first one scared the wits out of me. But it's gotten better. Britt only has them every few months now, usually after a very long day."

"Only every few months?" Jack said in obvious disbelief. "And what does she see?"

126

"It's always the same. Her parents are in a burning car, and she's trying to get them out."

Jack shuddered. He looked at her with pain-stricken eyes, and Lacey automatically took his hand, much as she would Britt's. "Did she really see that? I mean, did it happen that way?"

"No. None of us were anywhere near the car," she said. "After Beth and Kevin called us the last time, we waited and wondered why it was taking them so long. Then a policeman came to the door, and we found out." She leaned against the back of the sofa, feeling drained.

"That's brutal."

"You're right. I always saw them as this perfect family. They had everything. Four kids spaced exactly the way Beth wanted them. Their Christmas-card photos always looked like something out of Norman Rockwell." Suddenly it was too much, and Lacey could feel the tears seeping out from under closed lids. She wiped them away, but not before Jack had seen them.

His eyes were deep wells filled with agony. "You're too young and beautiful to be stuck with all this."

Lacey sat up. "I can accept it or not. Like it or not," she said sharply. "But whatever my decision, it will still be here."

"So you've decided to like it?" Jack looked as if someone had struck him over the head with a two-by-four.

"Most of the time. There are moments I want to pack a bag and move to Tahiti, preferably about two some afternoon when no one is home. They'd never find me." She gave a short laugh, filled with pain. "When I'm with you, I want to be free, free of everything. It isn't fair. I guess that's why it's so hard for me to let go around you."

Jack stroked her hair. "I'm sorry."

"Don't be. It's something I have to deal with." Lacey took off her glasses and set them on the end table near the couch. "I just have to shake off the feeling. I mean, what kind of kids would I raise if I hated every minute of raising them? There really is no alternative, Jack. Beth and I lost our mother to cancer when I was thirteen. Our dad turned me over to Beth a few years later as incorrigible...."

Jack looked incredulous. "You? Little Miss Perfect? Incorrigible?"

"Trust me."

"Right. What did you do, cheat in honors algebra?"

"How about I stole my dad's new car before I even had a license, took two friends and a bottle out partying in it, and ruined the paint job and other portions of the vehicle by going through the plate-glass window of the local bank, among other things."

Jack was wide-eyed. "Lady, never in a million years—"

"That's because I learned from the experience." Her laugh was shaky at best. Maybe she had learned too well, Lacey thought. Never would she be able to unrein herself again without thinking of the upheaval that bout had cost. Never could she be totally free without wondering what it was going to do to her, to the people around her.

Jack seemed to echo her thoughts. "You know, it is possible to have fun without running amok. You ought to try it once in a while." He stroked her hair.

Her smile was lopsided. "Maybe we can switch places. You're going to have to go through some of this too, you know."

"What do you mean?" Jack seemed truly confused.

"Kenton. I know he has a mother to raise him and all, but, Jack, he has grandparents. A grandma and a grandpa who don't even know he exists."

Jack's face was a tense mask. "You've got to be kidding. I couldn't do that."

"Jack, he's a child. A sweet little boy who probably for the life of him can't understand where his daddy went. Why deny him the only family he has left?"

"I don't think they're ready for that. They may never be ready for that," Jack said.

"That may not be your decision. In any case, you have a child who must be provided for." Lacey sat up on the couch and tucked her legs under her. "Switching back to being your financial adviser—"

"Oh, must you?" Jack said with a groan.

Lacey got very serious. "Yes, I must. This has to be taken care of. You need to set up some kind of trust fund or something if you're going to keep paying Kimberly. You just can't take it out of the business on the sly. The IRS is going to have a fit."

Jack scowled. "I was hoping they didn't have to know."

"You've got to be honest with them," Lacey told him. "There's no other way."

"So it's as simple as that? You just want me to set up some kind of fund outside the business to pay maintenance?" Jack looked relieved, and Lacey hated to burst his bubble.

"As your financial adviser, yes, that's as simple as it gets. However, as your friend there's more to it."

She put her arm around him gently. "I wasn't kidding about your parents. Jack, they need to know. That little boy is going to need all the relatives he can get. Why deny them the pleasure of watching him grow up?"

Jack's face looked like a storm was brewing. "What pleasure? I mean, first, I'm going to have to tell them that Jamie kept the whole thing from them to begin with. Lacey, they don't know all the gruesome details. As far as they know, Jamie was this wonderful person who lived a great life and had one tragic accident."

Lacey shook her head. "I bet they know more than you think. Parents usually do."

"Not mine. Lacey, my dad is sixty-nine years old, and my mom's not far behind and on blood-pressure medication. This might send them round the bend with the shock."

Lacey pounded a pillow. "Baloney. Jack, they need to know. And you're the one to tell them."

"What if I don't? You going to do my job for me?"

"Of course not." Lacey was shocked at the notion. "But I will be very disappointed with you."

"Then learn to live with disappointment, lady," Jack said, his eyes glittering.

Suddenly Lacey was too tired to keep this conversation going. "I've had plenty of practice."

Jack looked ashamed. "I didn't mean to get that rude. I know you've been through plenty. What made you take it all on in the first place? Wasn't there anybody else?"

Lacey shook her head patiently. "In Kevin and Beth's will, I was named guardian, and I intended to fulfill my responsibilities."

Jack shook his head. "Four years of those screaming bouts alone would have done me in."

"That's one of the funny things," Lacey said. "The night terrors didn't even start until eighteen months after Beth and Kevin died." There, she'd said it again. It was still a little death every time she said it. A little pang that turned her vibrant dark-haired sister into a memory instead. "Britt was so little, she didn't really understand anything at the time, except that one day she had parents and the next, they didn't show up anymore. Through the first year and more she was good. Too good."

Lacey sat quietly for a while, remembering. The older kids had shouted, fought, raged. But Britt had been a little angel, which had worried Lacey more than all the others' tantrums and screaming matches combined. Then the terrors had started. "At first it was every night or every other. I didn't get a full night's sleep for months. But the psychologist said it was her way of dealing with things. She should outgrow them or the need for them in the next year or so."

"I guess that's good news," Jack said with a bitter edge in his voice. "But it's the pits that a six-year-old child should have to have them, period." He rested his chin in his hand and leaned on the arm of the couch. Oops seemed to sense that he was sunk into a bad mood and ambled over, sitting still a few inches from Jack's shoulder.

When Oops was sure he'd gotten Jack's attention, he uttered one of his strange little cries and rubbed his chin and head all over Jack's hand. Jack chuckled and looked over at Lacey, questioning.

"That means, 'If you haven't got anything better to do than feel sorry for yourself, then feed me,'" Lacey translated.

Jack gave a full-fledged laugh. "I understand why it's hard to be a pessimist around here. Where are the treats?"

Fourteen

In the morning Brittany was her old self, cheerful and garrulous as ever. Lacey could hardly stand the bright chatter at the breakfast table. She had gotten to bed much later than usual, then stayed awake for over an hour before going to sleep.

Normally she kept pace with Britt at this hour, but today it was difficult. When everyone else had found other pursuits, Lacey lingered over a cup of coffee and Brittany sat beside her, still rambling away.

"It's a good thing we haven't invited anybody to my birthday party because I've changed my mind."

"Again?" Lacey suppressed a groan. "I warn you, Brittany Kaye—this is the last time. First it was going to be just cake and ice cream—"

"Too boring," Britt interjected.

"Then skating—"

"But I still fall down a lot, and that would be no fun at my own birthday party."

"And now you don't want the sleepover party with Katie and Elizabeth and the others?"

Britt shook her head, and for a moment Lacey saw a flash of distress. She leaned over the table and cupped Brittany's soft cheeks in her hands. "Britt, sweetie, you don't have to worry about the bad dreams like last night. I'm pretty sure you won't have one then, especially if I don't let the sleepover get out of hand."

"Like Katie's? Her mom even let us have a whipped-cream fight."

Lacey shuddered. "Definitely no whipped-cream fights. And no bad dreams; I can almost promise."

Brittany smiled. "That wasn't why I was changing my mind. I've just decided is all."

Lacey didn't suppress the groan this time. Brittany's decisions were legendary. Once she made a definite decision, there was no turning back. Lacey had never found a force on earth powerful enough to change Brittany's mind after one of her decisions. "Tell me all about it."

"Well, you did say seven is getting awfully grown up."

"That I did."

"So I've decided to have a grown-up party. I want the dress from Ivey's, the gold locket, and Jack."

"And Jack?"

"Sure. Just Jack, to take me out to dinner at a fancy restaurant. The kind with real tablecloths and everything. I can read the menu now, and I'm not an embarrassment."

Lacey sat, coffee cup halfway to her mouth, pondering this one. True, she had fueled the fire by talking about the grown-up nature of seven-year-olds. But that was when she and Britt were discussing the unsuitability of chewing on real gold locket chains while they examined the jewelry on their latest shopping trip. That grown-up nature didn't include dinners with Jack.

"Britt, Jack might not want to go with us. I can ask him...."

"Us?" Brittany's chin jutted out, and Lacey knew she was really lost now. "I just meant him and me. A very small party."

Now Lacey really did wish she'd stayed in bed. "We'll see. Let me talk to him, and then we'll see."

"Oh, boy," Britt sang, skipping away as if everything had arranged itself perfectly. Lacey poured herself the half cup of coffee that was left in the pot, wondering how she was going to phrase this request. She'd have to be quick about it, in any case. If she didn't give Brittany an answer by Tuesday, she knew from past experience that Brittany would just find a telephone book and start calling all the J. Daltons listed until she got the right one. "And to think I applauded when she learned to read," Lacey muttered over her coffee. This was going to be one interesting conversation.

Jack, of course, was delighted with Britt's birthday request.

They were sitting in the office discussing it, but Lacey didn't feel like she was getting through to him. "This is *all* she wants for her birthday. Just a dress, a locket, and dinner with you."

"And I'm touched," Jack said, getting out his date book at work Monday morning. "Her birthday is…?"

"Two weeks. March 15."

"Beware the Ides of March. For Britt it's fitting."

"All too fitting. Jack, I don't know how strongly I can stress how important this is to her.…" Lacey began. Jack stood up and gave her an exaggerated look of hurt that made him look like Tom Sawyer, boyish and sincere.

"You don't trust me," he accused.

"I trust you, most of the time."

"Then what am I doing wrong?"

"That's just what I mean, Jack. Sometimes you don't take things seriously. Right now I'm being serious, and this is a serious subject. And I expect serious treatment."

"Now I understand why those kids toe the line around you. I've got it, Aunt Lacey," he said, sliding her glasses up her nose. "I will be there, honest. Now can we get some work done around here?"

"We'll get more done if you don't do that again."

"Do what?" He still looked boyish and innocent.

"Push my glasses up. There seems to be an electrical current that connects when your finger meets the bridge of my nose."

Jack looked almost relieved. "At least it's not one-way then. I was beginning to think I had a short circuit."

So he felt it too. The knowledge rocked Lacey back in her seat. If he felt it too, then the constant little touches from Jack were more than a tease. It was sort of like a kid putting his finger close to a light socket, seeing how far he could go. Well, today she wasn't playing. "I need some more information from you to get the last of my figures done for the audit."

Jack groaned. "Let's get it over with while I still have the stamina."

It took all of Lacey's stamina not to tell Jack why she needed all the figures.

It wasn't just for the audit. She and Leona were ready to give him both barrels. It was bad enough that over the weekend she finally told him how she felt about Kenton and about setting up the trust fund. Now she was ready to tell him again what she felt more strongly every day: Jack needed to get out of the business of selling other companies' jewelry. The more she knew about Jack, the more doubts she had about springing their idea on him like this. But it had to be done. She pushed back her chair and headed for the front.

"I'm free for lunch today if you are," she told Leona, who suddenly looked like a cat watching a goldfish.

"Let me get my purse and tell Jackson to mind the counter," she said. Lacey smiled, thinking about how Jack would protest if he knew what the two of them were plotting over the lunch table. Once he found out, the man would never let them go to lunch together again.

~ ~ ~ ~ ~

Two days later they were ready. Lacey knew that to stay in this job she had to make this presentation. It was the only sensible way for the business to go, and she would never forgive herself if she didn't give Jack the hard sell on the idea. After all, she had already tried the soft sell the day of the photo shoot, and it didn't work.

She and Leona had a little money riding on this, money they had laid out for supplies for the presentation. A little money and a lot of self-respect. They had done spreadsheets and graphics to support their point, made some mock advertising pages, and worked up a cost analysis for the changes they wanted to make. And now both of them sat nervously in the office waiting for Jack to finish his coffee and amble across the street. Lacey stood up and ran her hands down the side seams of Jack's favorite black skirt.

"He would pick this morning to have a big, leisurely breakfast," Leona muttered, picking a piece of lint off his empty chair. It seemed like hours before the front door of the shop opened, the bell rang, and they could hear Jack's cheery whistle.

He was wearing those red suspenders that gave him such a jaunty air. Lacey's chest tightened as she watched him cross the threshold into the office. She could actually feel her heart leap when she looked at him. Seeing the bright red blossom in his lapel and the way one lock of hair drifted over his forehead, Lacey realized that she wasn't making this presentation simply because it was the financially responsible thing to do.

She was putting her job on the line because she wanted to see those red suspenders every morning. She wanted to see them when they were still drooping while Jack shaved, before he put on his crisp white shirt. Even knowing everything she did about him, Lacey didn't want just to share a business with Jack Dalton, she wanted to share a life with him. It wasn't just finances, it was love. "Heaven help us all," she whispered. He winked as he came toward her, and Lacey took it as a good sign.

Half an hour later, he wasn't winking. He wasn't doing anything at all except sitting in his chair in the office, tensely drumming his fingers on the spotless desktop.

She and Leona had really laid it on the line. They told Jack why he ought to overhaul his business and why they were just the people to help. They pitched their idea forcefully, arguing when necessary, and showing all the back-up paperwork. So far Lacey didn't feel it was making much impression on Jack. He didn't look interested. In fact, if he looked anything it was tense, bordering on angry.

"All right, say something," she said. "This isn't going over the way we'd hoped."

"Lacey, I've been real patient," he said. "I didn't say a word when this place became the model of efficiency instead of a pit. I haven't fought any of your persnickety little changes."

"Persnickety? How about financially responsible?" Lacey snapped, temper flaring. "We didn't go to all this trouble to be picky, Jack. This is for your own good."

Jack smacked his flat palm down on the desk with a sound that echoed off the cinder-block walls. "Look, I'm tired of hearing what a lousy manager I am. I'm sick of the constant little complaints about how I run my business."

Lacey sat down in the nearest chair. "Is that how you see this?"

"It sure is." Jack raked his hand through his hair, getting that one errant lock out of his face.

Leona looked at him and spoke softly. "Tell me honestly that you've enjoyed one moment of managing this store, Jack Dalton. I've watched you do it."

"That's not the point," he muttered, looking at the floor.

"Of course it's the point," Lacey argued. "It's exactly the point. You don't make any secret that you like designing jewelry, not keeping books. So design jewelry. Be the best jewelry designer in Florida. Make pieces that make everybody drool."

"And in the process trash my family business." The look he gave her was defiant.

"Don't trash it. Improve it. Make it into what only you can make it, Jack."

"But that would mean selling off a good portion of the stock here and going in a totally different direction."

"So?" Leona chimed in. "You're not comfortable going in this direction anyway."

"But this was Jamie's store, his concept." There was a note of anguish in Jack's voice that brought Lacey's head up.

"It was his idea," Lacey said, trying to stay calm while something in her chest told her what this argument was all about, at least for Jack. "But without him here to make it go, it's a drain on the business. Why do you feel like you have to keep running things this way, like some memorial?"

"Because if he hadn't listened to me, he'd be here himself to run it," Jack said. His voice was strangled, and Lacey didn't have time to get a good look at his face. In an instant he had vaulted out of the chair and through the door, and only the ringing bell over the front door of the shop served to remind her that he had been sitting there a moment ago.

She was still behind him. Jack kept walking faster, but Lacey was persistent. There was maybe half a block between them now, but Jack could tell without looking back that even in those heels and short skirt, she was keeping up. He'd stayed half a block ahead for six blocks now. Jack hoped Lacey was sweating as much as he was in the warm spring sunshine. Let her suffer a little for hurting him. It was apparent that she wasn't giving up, not after nearly a mile.

Not only was she not giving up, but she was gaining on him. Within a block, she caught up. Jack, walking fast, hands thrust in his pockets, didn't acknowledge her. But she was there, breathing hard and staying right beside him.

"There's a bench at the corner," Lacey said, puffing. "We sit. You talk."

"It's just as well," Jack said, trying to catch his breath. "We're about to run onto the golf course anyway." A block away he could see the golfers, mostly older folks, taking advantage of the gorgeous day to play a round.

She reached the bench and sat, leaning her head over the back and trying to catch her breath. "I've got a stitch in my side," she said, panting.

"Nobody asked you to follow me." Jack's voice sounded harsh even to him. The ragged edge to it had more to do with emotion than with being out of breath. He sat down on the bench, keeping plenty of distance between them.

"Okay, we're going to talk," Lacey said. "And if you walk away from me again, I'll follow you, just like the rabbit."

"I beg your pardon?"

"It's a family saying, I guess. Britt's favorite book is about a little rabbit who runs away from home, and every time he does, his mother follows after him. When she was five she threatened to run away from home, and I told her not to bother because I'd come after her, just like the rabbit."

"I'm not Britt, and I don't need a mother rabbit, Lacey." Jack's shoulders slumped as he leaned forward.

"I know that. But you do need to talk to someone. Do you really feel that Jamie's death was your fault?"

"Let's put it this way—if I hadn't issued an ultimatum, he'd still be walking around."

Lacey's silence forced him to go on. She sat still, looking straight into his eyes. He sat quietly for a minute and ran his hand through his hair.

"His problems were getting out of hand. He'd moved out of our apartment permanently, and I just figured at first it was to declare independence. I mean, we were both adults. Later I realized it was so he could go home from work and drink every night. Kimberly didn't object. Maybe she was too scared to." Jack looked at the golfers teeing up on a nearby hole, but Lacey could tell he didn't see them.

"After a while I knew things weren't being managed right. I was working my tail off, he was working his tail off, and we just weren't getting anywhere."

Jack felt very old and tired telling this story. It was the first time he had told anyone. "The morning I realized that it was not plain coffee he was pouring out of his thermos at 10:00 A.M. I told him he had two choices. He could find a treatment program someplace and check himself in, or I could call the rest of the family and get him removed from the business. Either way I was tired of looking out for him."

"And then what happened?"

Jack leaned his elbows on his knees. "He found a program. We went over together, checked the place out. It looked good. I agreed to give him two days, which he said he needed, to get things in order before he checked in."

Jack looked over the course. He could hear the distinct thwack of a club hitting a golf ball, and they both watched a portly older man in a floppy blue hat follow the progress of his ball onto the green. There was a little breeze that tugged at Lacey's hair, making her look no older than Becca. There were tears in her eyes, and Jack realized with a start that they were for him.

She reached out and took Jack's hand, and he grasped it like a lifeline as he continued the story. "He used those two days, but not to get anything in order. About four hours before he should have checked in, I got a call from the highway patrol. He'd run his car into a concrete abutment. Fortunately it was only a one-car accident and he was the only one in his car."

Jack could hear a bird in one of the trees nearby and the putt-putt of a golf cart. The sunlight was so hot on his face he almost wanted to brush it away.

Finally Lacey said something. "You are not responsible for your brother's death. Jack, if anything, you probably prolonged his life by covering up for him, looking out for him."

"But if I hadn't tried to force him into treatment, he wouldn't have had the drinking bout or the wreck."

Lacey eased her fingers out of his grip. She knelt in front of him, and Jack was about to tell her she was ruining her hose, but the look on her face stopped him. She was very determined as she put a hand on each of his knees, leaning into his face. "Prove it," she said softly.

Jack couldn't hear anything but the soft hum of the warm breeze around them. "What?"

"Prove it. Prove to me or anybody else, Jack Dalton, that your trying to get help for Jamie cost him anything that wouldn't have happened that night if you'd sat in the store and done nothing. Our lives, all of them, are in God's hands, Jack. We can seek the life he wants us to live and live it, or we can choose otherwise. It was Jamie's choices that night that led to his death, not anything you did."

The hum was inside his head now, rushing like Lacey's words. Jack was startled by the clarity of her face swimming through the haze he knew was caused by tears. He couldn't keep them all in anymore. With Lacey he felt safe to let them out anyway. "I guess you're right."

She used her thumb to smooth and dry his cheek and kept a hand on each side of his face. Lacey seemed to be using a lot of restraint to speak calmly and slowly. "I think I am. Jack, I was in counseling for a long time after Kevin and Beth died, just to deal with all my feelings. Trust me, you were not responsible. You need to talk about it, find some love and support to get it out of your system. And give it back to God."

Jack snorted. "Right. Love and support. Jamie is dead, and my parents only know there was a car wreck. You're the only one I've ever told this to, and I don't intend to try again. So, Lacey, who loves me enough to sit around and listen to this?"

"Jesus does, Jack. And I do too." The words were so soft. They seemed to surprise Lacey as much as they did Jack. She had an awed expression on her face, but she was smiling. Jack could feel himself smiling in response. He pulled her up beside him on the bench.

"You do?"

"Yes." She managed to get a little louder. "If you like, I can tell you once or twice a day until I convince you."

Jack brightened a little. "Every day?"

"Every day."

He grasped her shoulders, then wrapped his arms around her, squeezing her hard. It was like being thrown a lifeline. He held on until he realized Lacey was having trouble catching her breath. Then he eased up a little, felt her fill her ribcage with air, still close enough that he could almost feel both of their hearts beating. In the silence, Jack was aware that he hadn't heard a golf cart for a long time. He looked around.

The gent in the floppy blue hat was standing on the nearest green along with his partner, whose knobby knees protruded from truly awful Bermuda shorts. "Go ahead and kiss her, son," the man in the blue hat said with a grin. "We've seen it before."

Jack knew that at least one pair of golfers would have a good story to tell when they finished their round that morning. He personally made sure that it was a very good story. Maybe dipping Lacey over the bench like this was gilding the lily, but it would make for a much better tale, he was sure. And she didn't seem to mind a bit.

Fifteen

"I f we're going to make really distinctive stuff, we might as well market it right," Jack said, leaning on his worktable.

Lacey looked at him, his dreamy expression making her smile. He was moving ahead of her again, just like he had every day since she told him she loved him. "You mean go outside Orlando? Is this the same man who was totally against this idea two weeks ago?"

"Definitely. It's also the same guy that took only forty-eight hours to start the closeout sale on all the watches and stuff, remember?"

"All too well. You really caught me off guard with that one."

His answering smile was wolfish. "Not as off guard as that ice cube down your neck last night after basketball."

Lacey grimaced. "Don't remind me. You're not always the best role model for Brian, you know."

"Oh, I don't know, Lacey. At least he knows how to have fun," Jack said, tilting his chair back. "But back to business. With the right mailing list, we can get quite a clientele going."

Lacey leaned over him so that she was sure her words registered. "Then what are you going to do for staff? And where will you put them?"

"The ever-practical Lacey," Jack said, dropping a kiss on her forehead and sliding her glasses up the bridge of her nose. He grinned at her expression.

"Well of course," Lacey said, pursing her lips. "Somebody's got to think of it. The office part is easy. I mean, you own the whole building. We could always put the mail-order staff on the top floor."

Jack's chair went back to the upright position. "Ms. Robbins, the top floor, in case you haven't noticed, is my apartment."

"Yeah, but we're paying you well enough you could afford another place, Mr. Dalton. You can't lie to the accountant."

Jack rolled his eyes. "This is true. There were some advantages to not having a business manager, you know? Let me think about it. I'm pretty attached to that place. Besides, I feel like I've made enough changes for one month. Maybe for one lifetime."

"Oh no you don't," Lacey admonished. "I'll give you the month, but I won't let you claim a lifetime exclusion here. There will be more changes, Mr. Dalton. But we'll work hard to make them less painful."

"I hope so. I ought to get a medal for flexibility," Jack said.

"And that's what I like about you," Lacey said, trying to smooth his male ego. "You're so very flexible when you want to be."

"Just *like?* I should be hurt. I haven't heard the magic words today, and it's almost noon."

Lacey smiled. "I love you, Jack." As always, she waited for an answer. The right answer, the one she wanted to hear. Jack's saying, "And I love you too, Lacey."

As usual, that wasn't the answer. "I know. But I have to hear it," was what Jack actually said. Before Lacey could say anything in reply, Leona bustled up with more catalog page copy, and Jack was back into plotting and planning. Once he'd gotten enthusiastic about the design business, he and Leona had become a mutual-admiration society with their catalog.

Lacey shook her head and went back to her desk to try to get the last of the files that she'd pulled straightened out. This was the last batch of anything from the tired old file cabinets, and now everything else was in logical order. She still didn't look forward to the audit next week, but it was going to go as well as could be expected. The records weren't ever going to tell the story she would have wanted them to, but they were neat, clear, and in order.

No matter how many times she told him otherwise, Jack still couldn't believe that she truly enjoyed doing this. Most of the time Lacey hummed as she worked. And why not? Working for Jack was challenging and satisfying. She wasn't doing something that she'd done hundreds of times before. And as a wonderful bonus she got to look at Jack all day.

She had given up trying to hide her admiration. It didn't make much sense after she told him she loved him. Her actions might as well go with her words. So Lacey stopped trying to hide the fact, even when he was leaning over his worktable totally absorbed in making some piece of jewelry. He was at his best then. There was a fluid, peaceful quality to his movements that Lacey loved to watch.

Being openly admired appeared to be a new experience for Jack. He ate it up the way Oops inhaled chicken livers.

"You coming over tomorrow night?" Lacey asked the next time Jack strolled by her desk.

"Depends. What's on the menu?"

"Barbecued chicken. I ought to start charging you board, Dalton." Jack's coming over for dinner was getting to be more than a habit. The kids had gotten to the point where they set a place at the table for him every night, removing it if Lacey came in the door alone.

He fit in beautifully. Becca talked to him about music and consulted him on some of her wilder fashion ideas.

The next night, Lacey was thankful he had come when Becca tried out her newest idea. Lacey nearly choked on her chicken when she heard it. "A haircut how short?" She couldn't keep her voice from rising almost to a squeak.

Jack was shaking his head emphatically. "You've got the most beautiful hair, Becca. It looks like warm honey. Don't you dare hide it with some crew cut." He took a handful of it for emphasis as he stood over her. "Understand?"

"I guess so. But Sharon Phillips's mom let her...."

"I don't have to look at Sharon Phillips all the time, thank goodness," Jack said. "She probably looks like a goat chewed on her."

Becca wrinkled her nose and giggled, and the subject was closed. Lacey was amazed. If she had suggested the same things, World War Three would have erupted, and at her first chance, Becca would have appeared with a new, ghastly haircut. With Jack, a few words and a gentle touch of humor settled everything.

"You want to work some more on our game tonight?" Brian even wiped his mouth before he talked to Jack. Lacey wished she got the same respect, but then she couldn't help him with his history homework or win computer games like Jack either.

"Tonight it's Britt's turn first. Then a quick round, okay?"

If Brian was disappointed, he wasn't about to let it show. "Okay." He cleared his place at the table and slipped outside to shoot baskets. Brittany bounced in her seat, eyes shining.

Wherever Jack went in the house, he had two shadows. Oops and Brittany followed him everyplace unless he locked the door first. The cat adored sitting in his lap and batting at his gold cross if his shirt was left unbuttoned. Brittany just adored him, period. "Jack says..." became her all-purpose phrase. Surprisingly nobody teased her about it.

"So what's it going to be?"

"A story," Brittany said, predictably.

"Please," Lacey prompted getting up from the table. She turned to Jack. "If I have to read one more round of Britt's favorite book, I'm going to lose my dinner."

"Then aren't you glad I'm here?" Jack grinned as he walked up behind her.

She leaned against him briefly. "Delighted. Go read."

He read while Lacey checked Brian's homework; then they switched places, and she got Britt ready for bed while Jack and Brian played a round of their current computer game. They both seemed to enjoy it, judging from the noises coming from the office.

By the time they had finished, Lacey was coming out of her bedroom with bags and gift boxes. "Stay up here, and get ready for bed," she told Brian. "What you can't see, you can't tell about."

She balanced the boxes down the stairs and set them in the family room. There was actually tape on the roll in the kitchen for a change. Lacey wondered how it had escaped the kids. She shoved Oops into the bathroom and closed the door, much to his disgust.

Jack, coming down the hall, gave her a questioning look as she shut the door on the yowling cat. "He shreds paper," she explained as they walked into the family room. She got them both settled on the floor, setting several boxes on the floor in front of him. "Come give me a hand with these. I need at least one extra and maybe more to wrap them, especially the big one."

"Ah, the infamous dress from Ivey's," Jack said as he lifted the lid. Lacey stopped him quickly.

"You're not supposed to see that until Saturday night, I think. I've cut off all the tags, and there's no reason to open the box. Just help me wrap it."

Jack, with his artistic talent, got all the corners to fold right, and for once Lacey's packages didn't look like they'd been mutilated. All of them had large ruffly bows and crisp, shiny wrapping paper when they were done.

"Now what?"

"We go hide them in my closet behind the ironing board. No one ever looks there."

Jack helped her carry the boxes upstairs. "I'll be adding one to the stack."

"Oh?" Lacey reveled in the feel of his hands closing around her waist to help her down from the chair she perched on to hide the packages.

"Yep. And it's a surprise too. So there." His hands lingered at her waist for a moment, then let go with what felt like some reluctance. They both worked hard to keep some physical distance, even when the children weren't around.

"Let's go let Oops out of the bathroom. With him following me around looking at me cross-eyed, I'll be less tempted to sweep you into my arms." Jack moved one step closer and slid her glasses up her nose. "Someday, Lacey, I am going to take those off instead. I cherish the thought every time I slide them up."

Lacey gave a shaky laugh. "Well, keep cherishing the thought because we've got some difficult things to talk about." She hated to hit him with the rough stuff, but there wasn't going to be a better opportunity anytime soon.

The cat sprang out of the bathroom, grumbling, and stalked to the family-room couch. Jack sat down there, telling Oops what a wonderful beast he was. Lacey put all her papers on the coffee table and got Jack a fresh mug of coffee before she sat down. That should have tipped him off if anything did. Lacey had discovered that she only got domestic and maternal with

Jack when she was about to whack him over the head with a new idea he wouldn't like. He stayed blissfully unaware until she'd pulled out the whole folder of papers.

"What is all this?" he asked, sifting through it. "I thought you said no more changes for a while."

"No, Jackson, *you* said no more changes. *I* said I'd try to make them as painless as possible."

"And is this one? Painless?" he looked at her speculatively as she sat next to him on the couch.

"I hope so. It's the stuff for Kenton's trust fund. There was enough from the proceeds from the closeout sale after we started the new business fund, to set this up. I thought you could okay the paperwork, and then we could explain it to Kimberly."

Lacey could almost feel the tightness in Jack's cheek. The twitch of that one muscle came almost immediately. "I know this isn't easy, but it has to be done."

"Has to?" Jack's voice was as taut as his body.

"Well, should, anyway. We both agreed you can't just keep pulling money out of the business. If you're going to take Jamie's responsibility to his son seriously, we have to do this in a plain, legal fashion."

Jack was looking over the papers. "And this is about as plain and legal as it gets, isn't it?"

"It really is. Do you see any problems with it?" Lacey asked.

"Not really. The thought of explaining it all to Kimberly makes me cringe, though."

Lacey was ready for that argument. "If you want, I can go to Sanford and do this. As your financial manager."

Jack seemed relieved. "Would you? I can't seem to talk to her without getting into an argument."

"I'll do it—once. And while we're on the subject, let me get in my broken-record message, Jack. As much as this child probably needs the money, he needs people more. One woman cannot raise a child alone comfortably. Kenton needs you. And he needs his grandparents."

"Maybe someday," Jack said, closing the file and handing it back to Lacey. That seemed to close the subject for him. For Lacey it raised a little spine of aggravation that rubbed her the rest of the evening. It was still there when she walked Jack to the door later.

She took a shower once everyone else was in bed and the hot water came back. While she was sitting on the bed toweling her hair dry, Brooke called for a chat. She did that about once a week late at night when the rates went down. Lacey filled her in on how life was going. Most of it anyway, Lacey thought, listening to Brooke giggle a little.

"That sounds like things are getting intense, Aunt Lacey. When do I get to meet this guy?"

"Next time you're home. He'll be around, I hope," Lacey said, wondering even as she said it if it was true. She pushed the thought away.

"You hope? Are there problems?" Brooke asked.

"Not with me. But he just won't see things the same way I do, and it's so frustrating."

"How are your knees?" Brooke asked.

She sounded so much like her mother that Lacey swallowed her last gulp of iced tea the wrong way. "You got me," she said, gasping, when she got her breath back.

"Yeah, well, you didn't answer the question. And I am sorry I made you choke," Brooke said.

"I deserved it," Lacey told her. "And you're right, my knees could use more of a workout." Those had been Beth's code words to her for years when Lacey had complained about her problems, especially other people's stubbornness in not seeing things her way, the right way.

"How are your knees?" she could still hear Beth asking after one of her complaints. "They must be sore. Because if you've got time to complain to me about the way other people are doing things, it must mean you've taken it in prayer to Jesus already. And you know, once you've done that, they're not your problems anymore."

Getting the same prod from Brooke made her feel repentant. She hoped that would change the subject of the conversation. Quickly. She wasn't ready for this topic, she discovered. "Speaking of spiritual workouts, I know what was tops on your list. Do you still want me to come up for spring parents' weekend?"

"You could do that? With it happening in the middle of tax-season, I figured it was a lost cause."

"Now that I'm working for Jack, I've had to revamp my whole tax-season schedule anyway. I think we can figure something out," Lacey told her niece. They spent the rest of their phone conversation planning what to see in Atlanta and around the campus while she visited. For Lacey it was a welcome change from the subject they had been discussing before.

Brooke, of course, couldn't let it totally rest. "I've got to go study," she finally said. "And you've got to go work out."

"That I do," Lacey agreed with a sigh. "Thanks for reminding me. I love you."

"Love you too," Brooke said before she hung up. Lacey put the phone back in its cradle and slipped off her bed. No time like the present to start that workout.

Sixteen

J ack wasn't around much at work Wednesday. He claimed to be visiting Mrs. Dunwoody and other clients about custom orders, but Lacey had never seen him look quite so pleased with himself over any custom order before. Faraway and dreamy—just like Brian but not so cocky. He wasn't in the shop long enough that day for her to approach him and see what was going on.

Thursday morning she spent an hour running errands before work, trying to get ready for the big weekend. She was still playing telephone tag with Kimberly's answering machine, and there was no new message when she got into the store after ten. "If she calls and you're gone, I'll take the message," Leona said. "Jack seems so preoccupied this morning that I don't think he'd hear the phone anyway."

Lacey smiled. That was more like the Jack Dalton she knew and loved. She wondered what marvelous jeweled piece would result from this new current of artistry and creativity.

That night when she told him good-bye, he sat up, and the lights that went on behind his eyes showed that he was truly paying attention. He pulled her close and kissed her softly before she left.

Still, as she went home, changed, and started dinner for the kids, Lacey could still see him bent over his worktable, oblivious to the world, including her. That image disturbed her more than a little. Jack was so wrapped up in his work that Lacey was afraid he made it the cornerstone of his life.

She was in love with Jack. But she knew there couldn't be a lasting relationship between the two of them if his cornerstone really was work instead of Jesus. The thought nagged at her throughout the evening. It meant that for the first time Lacey wondered if Jack would find any wedding band too tight. Perhaps they could fashion one together that wouldn't be too constricting, even when added to children, a cat, and a business. More than once she whispered a silent prayer that it was God's will for them to build a relationship.

Somehow she suspected that Jack wasn't thinking along the same lines. She couldn't say what lines he was thinking along, but Lacey suspected it wasn't instant matrimony and years of commitment to a mortgage, several sets of braces, and beginning all over again with children of their own.

That was why Lacey was so surprised when the third or fourth phone call of the evening was actually for her. Becca handed the receiver to her, looking as surprised as Lacey felt.

"Hi, it's me. I just wanted to talk," Jack said. "I was thinking about you, and I wanted to apologize for snapping at you the other day about the apartment. I've tried to take most of the changes you've suggested like a good sport because I know you have my best interest at heart, but this one is hard. I'm so settled here."

"I bet you are. I can understand how you feel, Jack. I hate moving," Lacey said, looking around the kitchen. She couldn't imagine trying to uproot this gang again. The refrigerator art and magnets alone would take a day to sort through and pack.

The conversation continued, light and inconsequential. Lacey polished countertops and unloaded the dishwasher while she talked. Hearing Jack's voice gave her an inspiration.

"What do you say we try for breakfast tomorrow morning? Britt goes to choir practice before school, and the older two are on the bus by seven-thirty anyway. Want to give it a shot?"

"Can't," Jack said succinctly. "I already set something up

with the Dunwoodys." Then he said good-bye and they hung up. Lacey couldn't explain why she felt so empty. She hadn't really expected Jack to profess eternal love on the telephone, even tonight. She opened the cabinet next to the sink and got out the cleaning supplies. It was time to work off some frustrations.

Lacey was still working on the downstairs bathroom when the phone rang again half an hour later. Brian and Becca both raced to different extensions, and she pitied whoever was on the other end. When Brian came into the room and announced that it was another call for her, Lacey nearly dropped the scrub brush. Two calls in an evening had to be a record.

The woman's voice on the other end was soft and tentative. "Ms. Robbins? I'm Kimberly Thompson. You've been leaving messages for me?"

Lacey took a deep breath and pushed her glasses up, thrusting away the picture of Jack removing them as quickly as it entered her mind. "Yes, well, I'm the business manager for Dalton Jewelry now, and I've got some business to discuss with you."

"Business? You mean I've been elevated to such official status that now I'm business? I'm impressed." The ironic tone told Lacey that this woman thought just as highly of Jack as he did of her.

"We do need to get together, Ms. Thompson," Lacey said, trying to keep her voice even.

"I'm sure we do. Can we do it Saturday? I can't have personal visitors at work, and I refuse to keep Kenton in day care any longer on a weekday just to discuss Jack Dalton's 'business.'"

Lacey sighed, thinking of everything she already had planned for Saturday to get ready for Britt's birthday. But she'd told Jack she'd do this, and if Saturday suited Kimberly, it would have to suit her too. "Sure. It won't take long."

"If Jack's involved, I'm sure it won't," she said. She gave Lacey instructions on how to find her apartment, and they hung up. As she put down the phone, the nagging doubts Lacey had begun to admit to nibbled even harder at the edges of her confidence.

It was almost a relief that Jack was still out with the Dunwoodys when Lacey got to work. Between the audit coming up and Britt's birthday, she was going to be so busy that there wouldn't be much time for him.

For the first hour, she was so busy arranging her paperwork for the upcoming audit that she couldn't worry about anything else. And when Jack came in, it was only to drop a quick kiss on the back of her neck. "Hi, you," he murmured, not really stopping for an answer before he went upstairs for coffee. Jack had never kissed her hello in the morning before. Like all of his kisses at any time of day, this one made her tingle. It didn't reassure her, though, or calm any of her fears. Somehow it made Lacey even more on edge than she had been before.

Vaguely she heard Jack take a phone call, and then he disappeared. "One of Mrs. Dunwoody's friends with another order. Jack says this could be the launch of the specialty jewelry business in earnest," Leona said.

As each hour passed and Jack still hadn't put in enough of an appearance for them to talk, Lacey got more nervous. She needed to talk to Jack. She wanted to reassure herself that he would be solid and stable for a change, able to provide the things she needed right now. Even if there wasn't any discussion of where they would go from here, there was the immediate issue of his "date" with Brittany. That had to be taken care of.

Five o'clock came, and Jack was still barricaded upstairs, where he'd been without a word ever since he came back from his midafternoon appointment. It gave Lacey uneasy feelings to have to climb the stairs and rap on the door, her briefcase in hand.

"Come in." Jack's voice sounded far away. When Lacey went in, she could see why. His desk was surrounded in paper ankle deep, and there were design drawings on every surface. "What can I do for you?" Jack asked without looking up.

Aggravation flared, but Lacey tried to keep it in check. "Tell me what day it is."

"Friday. March 14. Approximately twenty-six hours before I am to take a certain seven-year-old out to dinner," Jack said, still sketching. "I haven't forgotten, Lacey."

"I know that, Jack." Lacey ran her fingers down the door frame. "It's just that…I guess I'm never sure where you are when you get that creative look in your eye."

Jack shook his head. "Honestly, Lacey, I know you think I'm the most unreliable soul in the world, but sometimes I remember. Until then, let me design this piece of jewelry. It's the second custom order I've gotten in three days, and I'm on a roll."

"Fine," Lacey said. She walked over to the desk and kissed the top of his head, inhaling the crisp, warm scent of him. It was all she could do without breaking his concentration. She drove home, still more than a little worried.

Jack was an adult, and she couldn't ride herd on him like she did the kids. But Lacey got the feeling he just didn't understand how important it was to show up on time tomorrow night, looking good and ready to go. For Britt and for her. She hoped that he didn't get so caught up in something that he lost track of time.

The thought was still with Lacey in the morning as she

crammed as many of her Saturday errands as she could into a third of the usual time. She made it through the dry cleaners and the hardware store in record time and allowed herself a quick stroll through the farmers' market in Winter Park.

The triangular lot was full of flowers and produce this time of year. She got a quart of strawberries from her favorite vendor and some of the first asparagus of the season. At least while Britt was having an elegant dinner with Jack, the rest of them would be eating well too.

Once her basket was full, she went inside to pick up Britt's favorite chocolate masterpiece from the "cake lady." Nothing she could bake was that good, so she had given up trying. Everything purchased, she zipped back to the car and loaded up the trunk.

Nothing would spoil while she made the trip to Sanford and back. Nothing but her patience. As she got closer to meeting Kimberly, with her obvious disdain of Jack and the Daltons in general, Lacey got more and more tense. She didn't want to hear anything right now that would make her worry more about Jack, but she suspected that would be exactly what she'd get.

The apartment was small but clean, if sparsely furnished. The woman sitting across the kitchen table looked even younger and smaller than Lacey remembered. Kenton was a normal, active two-year-old. A bundle of blond energy, he alternated between climbing up his mother's leg and watching the *Noah's Ark* video she put on the television.

Kimberly reminded Lacey of a forest animal. The nimbus of blond hair and the doe eyes gave the impression of something frightened that might bolt any minute. Kimberly held her ground, however, as Lacey explained the paperwork. Her eyes got even larger as she sat, trying to digest it all.

"You got Jack Dalton to do this? How? That man hates me." Lacey tried to say something, but Kimberly went on with a wry laugh. "No, don't deny it. I can't blame him for the way he feels. If anything I'd blame Jamie for the way he left things. But that wouldn't do any good.

"I stopped blaming Jamie a long time ago. For Jamie there was always going to be time tomorrow to do what needed to be done. I knew that living with him wasn't right, but it was temporary. We were going to get married. Even after the baby came, he had such big plans. Then finally his tomorrows ran out."

Kimberly's words ran out for a while then too. Lacey could only reach out to her and pat her hand. "The Bible says none of us know when our life is going to end. That's why we have to live each day in the Lord."

Kimberly gave a wry smile. "I know. And when I met Jamie, I had been away from the Lord for a long time. After he died the couple next door was so good to me. And they took me to their church and got me to talk to the pastor about all the anger I was feeling toward Jamie—and God."

Kenton seemed to sense that the conversation had taken a serious turn. He bounded up to his mother, climbed into her lap, and patted her face. "Mama, you sad? Want me to sing to you?"

The action of that chubby little hand, each knuckle still dimpled in the way of babies, tugged at Lacey's heartstrings. It made Kimberly smile as well. "No, sugar. I'm all right."

She looked down at her cup of coffee and eased Kenton onto the floor again. "Go watch your movie, sugar, just for a minute or two, okay?" She watched him go, shaking her head. "He doesn't know what to make of me actually telling him to watch TV. Usually it's forbidden fruit. After spending as many hours as he does at day care, I try to read to him on Saturdays, or we run errands together." She looked over at the active little body bouncing in front of the television. Lacey could feel the love in that look.

"He's a handful, I bet," Lacey said. "I remember that age. Has he gotten to 'why' yet?"

Kimberly nodded. "With a vengeance. Including lots of whys I can't answer, like why the other kids at school have two people that pick them up sometimes and people to come on grandparents' day." She looked up at Lacey. "You said you're Jack's business manager. No business manager would do this, even for somebody as persuasive as one of the Dalton brothers."

Lacey could see that there was more adult resolution behind Kimberly's brown eyes than she had seen there before.

"There's more to it than that," she admitted. "I don't know how much more yet. Maybe a lot."

Kimberly's mouth turned up in one corner. "Be careful. Jack's more like Jamie than he'd like to admit. Not the drinking or anything. That was part of Jamie that was just Jamie. But Jamie couldn't ever handle the tough stuff, not for long. And when I look at Jack, those same eyes look back at me in a different face."

Kenton ran up again. He wanted a glass of juice, and his mother adroitly poured it, settled him at the counter on a stool, and signed the papers.

That serious action seemed to work on her bouncy son the way a telephone call would, riveting his attention to his mother and making her irresistible. "Mom? Mom? Mom?" he caroled, scooting off the stool and tugging at her arm.

"What, Kenton James? I can answer you, but please don't pull on me while I'm writing, okay?"

"Okay. But I gots a question," he said.

His mother finished signing the sheet in front of her and looked at him. "Okay, what's the question?"

"How big is God?"

His earnest query startled both of the adults into laughter. "How big do you want him to be?" his mother asked, sweeping him up in her arms as he giggled.

"Heee-yuge," Kenton laughed. "Big, big, big."

"Well, you're in luck, then, because that's how big he is," his mother told him. "Huge. Humongous. And all of that humongousness loves you."

"Cool," Kenton said with a grin and squirmed down. "I gotta finish my juice."

Lacey gathered her papers as Kimberly stood up. "I don't want to keep you. And we've got errands to run, Ms. Robbins. If I'm out of line talking about Jack, I'm sorry, but I've spent too much time saying nothing when I should have said something, and maybe now I'm starting to change."

The hand Lacey shook was firm and cool and competent, and Kimberly's words echoed in Lacey's mind all through the day.

Seventeen

Dread and dismay made a knot in Lacey's stomach. *This can't be happening,* Lacey told herself for the tenth time. Jack would not just leave them in the lurch like this. It was long past seven, and he hadn't come, hadn't called. Surely he would show up soon, even though nobody answered at the store, nobody answered at the apartment, and he wasn't pulling up to the front door. Kimberly's words danced like demons in her head, adding to her own doubts as it got later and later.

No one noticed the decorations Lacey had spent an hour hanging. The pink and silver streamers looked out of place. The big helium balloon was already drooping, as if it sensed the mood in the room. Her family in the living room looked like a still life.

Brian had one leg flung over the arm of the couch, and the cat lay motionless on the cushion over his head. Becca was sitting in her favorite chair, rigid as a statue of a teenager. Lacey was the only one moving. She paced back and forth in front of the window like a caged tiger.

She felt like curling back her lip in a feline snarl. How could Jack have done this? *Why, Lord, why?* she asked silently, still pacing. She went into the kitchen and punched Jack's number into the phone. When it rang ten times with no answer, she tried the shop number. When it rang and rang with no answer, she slammed the phone down.

Back in the living room, no one had moved. "Now what time is it?" asked Britt plaintively.

"Five minutes after you asked last time," Becca snapped.

"That makes it seven twenty-five," Brian piped up.

Lacey didn't say anything. She looked at Brittany sitting in a chair, ankles crossed, trying not to put a run in her brand-new tights. She was a picture. Her hair cascaded in curls it had taken half an hour to fix. The skirt of her ruffled dress spread its flounces about her making her look like she was sitting in the middle of a flower. Earlier, Becca had polished Britt's nails for her and loaned her a spritz of perfume.

She looked very much the lady. Except that ladies' lower lips do not tremble quite like Brittany's was beginning to.

"He's not coming, is he?" she said in a tiny voice.

"I'm afraid not, Britt. Would you like to do something else instead?"

She shook her head. "I'll wait for a little while longer, I think."

Ten minutes later the tears began to come. Lacey gathered her up and let Brittany cry burrowed into her neck for a few minutes while in her mind she railed at Jack. If he had just hurt her, it would be different. She was tough and resilient, and she would mend. But to hurt one of her kids was unforgivable.

When Britt's crying had subsided into hiccups, Lacey pulled her back and used a tissue to wipe her streaked face. "Let's not let this ruin your birthday entirely, okay?"

"But he didn't come."

"I know. And if there was any way I could make him appear right here, right now, I would. But I can't." She smoothed down the front of Britt's hair, where the curls were threatening to tangle. "What I can do is suggest an alternative."

Britt, on the trail of a new word, stopped sniffling. "What's that?"

"Something else to do instead. Instead of sitting here in the dark in the living room all night, waiting, why don't we go out and have ice cream for dinner?"

Britt cocked her head, thinking. "Can I have anything I want?"

Lacey nodded. "And afterward we'll come back here for cake and strawberries for dessert."

"Okay. I guess that will do." It was the best Lacey could hope for. "But let me go change clothes. I don't want to get fudge sauce on my new dress."

Becca went upstairs with her. "Come on. Since it's your birthday I'll let you borrow my new shirt. We'll tie it on the side like a tunic, and you'll look really cool."

Ten minutes later they bounded down the stairs. Britt did indeed look really cool. Or at least she would in the eyes of most fourteen-year-olds, and it obviously thrilled her silly. Lacey thought the tunic over her tights was cute, and the curly ponytail pulled to one side gave her a jaunty look. She decided to ignore the swipe of clear lip gloss Becca had added and let them both think they were getting away with something.

Nobody begrudged Britt the front seat on the way to the ice-cream parlor, and for once Lacey was terribly proud of her children. Both of the older two were being as tactful and pleasant as they knew how to be to their sister. And it was working.

Britt ordered a gloppy concoction with every topping in the store on top of her usual vanilla. While she dug in, sitting at one of the counter's high stools, a fast-moving blond blur leaped up onto the next stool. "Hi, Britt. Whatcha got?" Lacey had never been happier to see one of Britt's friends.

"The Belly Buster. Bet you couldn't eat one by yourself, Tyler."

"I can eat anything," the boy said smugly.

"He can, too," his mother said in a tired voice. "At least four times a day. If he eats like this now, how am I going to feed him in a few years?"

"You spend a lot of time buying bread, milk, and hamburger," Lacey said, ruffling Brian's hair as he grimaced.

Britt and her friend chattered on and on, eating their ice cream. Finally they both finished the gooey messes, and Britt slid off her stool and walked over to Lacey's table, patting her stomach. "Can I have a quarter for the video games? Tyler thinks he can beat me."

"Wish him good luck," Lacey said, putting two quarters in her hand. "Happy birthday."

"Is it really your birthday, Brittany? I guess I'd better let you win once, huh?"

As Tyler dashed for the machine, Britt leaned over to Lacey. "Isn't he cute? He's in my class at school, and Friday he drew on my math paper. I think he likes me." She skipped off to challenge her friend at the machines, and Lacey smiled weakly. Another one growing up so fast it made her head spin.

Finally Lacey was able to get Britt away from the machines with the promise to have Tyler over some afternoon after school. "I'll beat you then, too," she said, giggling, as they left the video games.

In the parking lot next to the car, Britt shrieked and bent down quickly, waving something as she popped up. "Five dollars! I found five whole dollars!" She whooped in triumph. "With the money in my bank and my birthday money from Grandma Horton and this, I've got enough money to buy the game I want. It really is my lucky day after all."

Lacey felt tears sting the insides of her eyelids and forced them to stay there unshed. She thanked heaven for Britt's resiliency again. "I guess it is," she managed to say. And Jack

Dalton's name was mud. No, worse than mud. Slime.

Britt stood in the parking lot, still grinning. "I should go into the grocery store and see if anybody lost this. Somebody might need it to buy milk for a baby or something." She was so earnest and serious about it that Lacey agreed, and they headed to the store.

Halfway up the aisle, they met an older gentleman walking in their direction, head down. "Are you looking for something? Did you drop some money?" Brittany asked him.

"I did. A five-dollar bill," he said.

"Then this is yours," she said, holding it out to him. "The wind blew it in front of my car door. I found it."

He looked at her, eyes widening in amazement. "And you came into the store to look for whoever lost it?"

Britt shrugged. "Sure. I thought somebody might need it to buy milk for a baby or something."

The man chuckled. "More like dog food, but that mutt thinks he's my baby." He took the money that Brittany held out to him. "And I think this kind of honesty ought to be rewarded. Can I give her a finder's fee, Mom?" he asked, looking at Lacey.

"That's up to you," Lacey told him, her pride in Britt growing.

"It's my birthday," she informed the man as he got out a battered brown wallet. "We just had ice cream for dinner."

"That sounds like a birthday thing to do," he said, handing her a bill.

She looked at it and looked back at him. "Is this real?"

"Sure is. Never seen one before?"

Britt shook her head and showed the bill to Lacey. "Nope. Never have."

"It's a two-dollar bill," the older gentleman told her. "And it's real. Happy birthday, and thank you so much."

"You're welcome. Thank you for my birthday present." Britt skipped back to Lacey, and they headed for the car.

"You did well," Lacey told her.

"Know what the good part is? I think even with this two dollars instead of the five dollars, I still have enough for my game cartridge."

Lacey stroked her head as they reached the car. "The good part is that you found the owner."

An hour later, Brittany was in bed, snuggled under the covers, her hair down, waiting patiently for Lacey to read her a bedtime story. Lacey didn't even groan as she picked up the book and stretched out on the bed next to Britt. It was her birthday, and Lacey would read her favorite book cheerfully.

"Three stories. No more," she said firmly, opening the book of fables. She could have recited the one about the lion with the thorn in his paw by memory, but she turned the pages in front of her like a conscientious story reader instead. For the one about the boy crying wolf she even managed to insert a little emotion, silently thinking of an apartment in downtown Winter Park where she'd like to put that wolf for an hour.

She even made it through Britt's personal favorite without droning. The grasshopper and the ant. The diligent, hardworking little ant looked like such a drudge. "Just like 'Ant' Lacey," she muttered to herself as she turned a page.

"Hmm?" Britt said sleepily.

"Oh, nothing much," Lacey said, reading on. "'And then winter came. The cold winds blew and it began to snow.'"

"Then the grasshopper got into his convertible and headed for the beach, and the ant stayed in the snow and got stepped on," Britt said with a grin. "That's the way Jack told it. Isn't that funny?"

"It sounds just like Jack," Lacey said, trying to smile.

"Birthday or not, I think it's time to hear prayers and say good night."

Brittany's prayers tended to ramble. She talked to God naturally, as she would have talked her earthly father had he been around. Sometimes, in fact, she passed on messages to Kevin and Beth. Tonight was no different. "Thanks for everything. I really had a nice birthday. And the two-dollar bill is really cool. And please bless Jack, and help me forgive him tomorrow if he calls. Guess that's about it. Amen."

The lump in Lacey's throat was big enough to choke her. "Amen," she whispered after Britt. She kissed the girl good night and headed out of the room.

In the hall it sounded like a normal night. Becca's radio was as loud as she dared play it once Britt was asleep, and the handset to the cordless phone in the hall had vanished. In the office there was a green glow that told Lacey Brian had taken over her computer.

So the grasshopper got into his convertible and headed for the beach, did he? Lacey clenched her fists and tried not to put one of them through the wall. This was one ant that nobody was going to step on again. Especially in the heart region. Maybe Britt could ask to forgive Jack quickly and easily, but it would be a while before Lacey could ask God to forgive Jack.

Jack Dalton could take his sports car and head for the beach, but it was going to be without Lacey. This time she was finished.

Sunday morning was usually Lacey's favorite time of the week. It was nice to get up slow and lazy and linger over the paper with a pot of coffee. Nobody wanted more than a bowl of cereal before church because the usual routine after services was for

168

Lacey to fix a big brunch so everybody could sit around talking and eating. It was the one time of the week no one argued over whose turn it was to load the dishwasher.

So naturally they would expect something better than the store-bought donuts Lacey felt like providing this morning when her feet hit the floor. Even the nubby beige carpeting felt too prickly today, and the sunshine was much too bright coming in the window. Of course a few more hours of good sleep might have changed her perspective.

The face that looked back at her in the mirror didn't look any better than she felt. Her hair was limp, and there were little bluish circles under her eyes. "Lovely," she told the haggard visage staring back at her. "Aren't we a vision this morning."

A hot shower improved her disposition if it didn't do much for her looks. The circles were there, and there just wasn't any way to hide them. So Lacey didn't even try. Somehow this morning the effort was beyond her anyway.

She padded down to the kitchen barefoot and looked through the refrigerator. Eggs, cheese, a loaf of bread, milk. Unfortunately everything was there for her usual big brunch fixings. There wasn't any reason to alter the routine at all. She stirred up an egg casserole with ham and put it in the refrigerator, ready to bake when they got home from church.

Britt came down wearing her new dress, and even Brian had put on an ironed shirt and khakis without being told. Lacey went back upstairs, dressed quickly, and was downstairs and ready to leave about the same time Becca was.

Brittany got several belated birthday wishes at church. Lacey was glad Britt was the focus of attention and no one among her own friends noticed how awful she looked. They went home right after services, and she popped the egg casserole into the oven and went upstairs to change into leggings and a shirt. As the smells began to drift up the stairs, bodies began to drift down for lunch.

Lacey decided she must look as awful as she felt. Nobody got her up from the table for anything during the meal. They all got their own milk, napkins, and anything else they needed without protest, a sure sign that it was "be nice to Aunt Lacey day." She wondered how far she could take it.

She needed to find action to work off this tremendous feeling of frustration. If she sat around the house waiting for Jack to call with some lame excuse, she'd probably punch a hole in the wallboard. "I'm going to go to the rink and work out for a while. Anybody else coming?"

Becca shook her head. "I've got homework to do, thanks."

It was all Lacey could do not to reach over and feel Becca's forehead to see if she was sick. She looked at the younger kids. "You guys?"

Brittany smiled sweetly. "If you'll take me by the store first and let me buy my game cartridge, Brian and I will just stay here and play it. That way I can beat him."

Brian hooted. "We'll see about that, shrimp."

Britt stuck out her tongue. "Will so beat you."

Before things escalated, Lacey cut them off. "Be ready by the time the dishes are done and it's a deal."

By the time Lacey pulled the stopper on the sink, Britt was standing in the kitchen, purse in hand. Lacey took her to the store, and they got the game cartridge so that no one would bother Becca while she did her homework. That, of course, involved use of a telephone (with a deeper voice on the other end that Lacey suspected was Eric) and a two-liter bottle of diet soda.

"I'll be back by three," she told the people in the family room. In case the blank stares facing the television screen as they zapped frothing bubbles was an indication that they might not be listening, Lacey left them a note. Then she drove the van to the roller rink.

The pulsating music washing over her was like a tonic. She tightened her rental skates as firmly as she dared over the ankles and flexed all her leg muscles. It felt good to push off and go gliding around the rink. As she picked up speed, she lost herself in the motion and the music.

Here she could think without the tears coming. She could detach herself enough to wonder what she should do next about Jack and work and everything.

In an hour she got a lot of thinking done. Lacey was surprised that she was dripping with sweat by the time she plopped down on a bench for a drink. After resting for a few minutes, she tossed the cup, empty now except for rattling ice, into the trash and pushed herself out onto the rink again.

Her muscles protested, but her mind still needed the workout. After four more songs, going around the rink at good speed, she looked at her watch with a start. It was nearly three. She had to shuck off her skates and get home or Britt, with her imagination, would concoct some horrific reason why she was late.

All her muscles protested when she sank down onto the bench to remove the lead weights with wheels attached to her feet. As she bent over to slip the left skate off, hands closed in on her shoulders from behind. Very familiar hands with callused palms and a gentle touch.

Lacey turned. There was Jack, black jeans and mirror shades making him fit right in with the crowd here. He looked like the adolescent she would have called him right now.

"You're late," she said. "By about eighteen hours."

"I know. No excuses," Jack said.

"None for me, definitely. I'm not the one who needs them. It's Britt you need to talk to."

"Already done. How do you think I found out you were here?" He shifted his weight and sat down next to her. "We had a consolation ice-cream cone at a haute cuisine spot with golden arches. After some talking, she decided to forgive me." The grin on his face was devastating. But today it only made Lacey angry.

"Great. One fast-food fix and everything is supposed to be all right, huh? What do we do now, Dalton?" She tried to keep her voice even so she wouldn't cause a scene.

"I was thinking we might get married," Jack said, pushing his sunglasses up on his hair. One look at those hazel eyes told Lacey he was serious. The heavy skates slithered out of Lacey's numb fingers, hitting the floor with a thud.

Eighteen

re you out of your mind?" Lacey's voice rose. She wasn't worried about making a scene anymore. Not with this lunatic standing next to her.

"Never been more sane," Jack said, leaning over as if he was going to kiss her.

"No," she said, pushing him away.

"Too public?"

"Too everything. I wasn't just saying no to a kiss, Jack. I was saying no, I won't marry you."

He looked stunned. "You won't? Why not?"

"Jack Dalton, have you lost it?" So the whole roller rink could hear—for once Lacey was not worried about making a scene. "You stood me up last night. No, worse, you stood my seven-year-old niece up last night. Now you waltz in here and say 'marry me' as if that's supposed to solve everything."

"It is. I messed up. I don't want to mess up again. I'm tired of having to go over to your place to explain things to you when I mess up. If we lived under the same roof, I could mess up in much closer proximity."

Jack's grin faded when he saw how angry Lacey was. "Okay, so maybe I'm a little bit blunt."

"A little bit blunt? You're not catching on, are you, Dalton? I will not marry you now," Lacey said in a shrill voice as her finger in the center of his chest backed him almost over a bench. "I will not marry you later. I would not marry you if you were the last man in Orlando. I do not want an undependable, immature, promise breaking—"

"I get the picture," Jack said, rubbing the middle of his

chest. "Would it help any if I said I had good reasons for not being there last night?"

"Name one good enough," Lacey said, her eyes narrowing and her chin jutting forward. "Other than hospitalization or death, I can't think of too many, and you're still walking around."

"How about helping out a client whose husband was passed out cold on the floor in the next room? How about getting said client and said husband, after several cups of coffee and a lot of soul searching, to go check out the treatment center I'd found for Jamie?"

"Mrs. Dunwoody? And Mr. Dunwoody?" Lacey sat down hard on the bench behind her. "Jack, he's one of the most prominent businessmen around town."

"Alcoholism doesn't play favorites, Lacey. Apparently one of the reasons he's been footing the bill for all these expensive little goodies has been a way of apologizing for his increasing lapses of memory, spells of 'not feeling well,' and the whole ball of wax."

"Don't they have a telephone?"

"If they do, they hide it well. I wasn't about to go looking for it for the first hour after I got there, and by the time things were squared away, it was awfully late. I knew Britt wouldn't be up that late, even on her birthday." He shoved his hands into his pockets and rocked back on his heels.

"Okay, so you were doing a good deed. But, Jack, you already had a good deed to do."

"I know, Lacey. But this one couldn't be put off. I've been skirting this issue with Mrs. Dunwoody for weeks. She's given me vague hints that her husband has problems. And you've been at me so much about taking responsibility for things that I figured you'd want me to do this." He struck a pose that reminded Lacey of Brian. "So am I forgiven?"

174

"Not really," Lacey said, trying to pull her face out of a colossal pout. "You could have called, at least to say that you'd come today. I'm glad you were doing a good thing, but, Jack, you already had a good thing to do. And you didn't do it."

"And now you're feeling abandoned," Jack said softly. "If I'd given that more thought, I would have done something about it, Lacey. You've been abandoned before, and you figure I'm just one more person doing it."

Lacey looked at the gray carpet under her feet. She flashed back to the tired, knowledgeable look on Kimberly's face the day before. "Maybe that's part of it. All I know is that right now I'd have a hard time trusting you. And I certainly couldn't marry somebody I didn't trust. A proposal today is way out of line." She looked at him, and her eyes misted over. "I couldn't work with somebody I didn't trust either, Jack."

"What are you saying?" His face looked troubled.

"That I think I ought to go back to being a tax accountant. I've been thinking about it since last night, and I think this is for the best. Don't worry, I'll show up for the audit Monday. I keep my promises," Lacey knew how harsh that sounded, and right now she didn't care. "But after tomorrow, find yourself a new business manager. One that doesn't mind when you get into your convertible and drive off to the beach." She picked up the skates and walked away, turning in her skates at the counter and putting on her shoes.

Balancing on one foot while she slipped on a moccasin, Lacey prayed that Jack wouldn't follow her. Not now, while she was still off balance both physically and mentally. Now if he came after her, put his arms around her, started giving her sweet promises or even sweeter kisses, her resolve to walk away would crumble.

She got out of the rink and into the van alone. There was

no one following her, no one at all. As glad as Lacey was that that was the case, she was somehow sorry at the same time.

Monday morning Lacey got up early and got everyone ready for school. By the time she sent them off, she was so tense she felt like a glass statue. One wrong turn and she was going to hit a sharp corner and shatter. She had to concentrate. This was not the frame of mind to have when facing an audit meeting with an IRS field agent.

She got out her blue suit and a plain white shell. Might as well look like the competition, she told herself. She smoothed her hair back conservatively and put on delicate earrings. Even with red glasses, the face looking back at her in the mirror was that of a dedicated accountant. "Boring, boring, boring," she caroled, applying a touch of blush. She needed something to mask the pallor this morning. And some cover for the raccoon circles under her eyes. This had not been another stellar night's sleep.

At nine she got in the car, drove to Park Avenue, and parked in one of the municipal lots. This morning her briefcase felt heavy. Even Jack's new window display of bright, unique items didn't catch her eye.

Leona looked up when the bell rang and Lacey walked in. "You look like five miles of bad road," Leona said, grimacing. "You coming down with the flu?"

"No, just a heavy case of reality," Lacey said. "I'll tell you about it later when you have time, like maybe an hour or two."

Leona gave a quirky smile. "I think I've already heard one chapter of this story. Jackson's back up in the apartment taking a shower. When I got here he was already messing around at the workbench. From the looks of it, he may have been down here all night."

If that was supposed to bring a pang of sympathy to Lacey's

heart, it was a poor bid. So he couldn't sleep either. At least for Jack it was profitable.

Lacey got her records out of the file cabinet and spread them on the desk in neat stacks in the order she suspected the field auditor was going to want them. She took a deep breath and walked over to Leona's coffeepot. "Help yourself," Leona called when she saw Lacey standing in front of it. "I figured this would be at least a two-pot day. I even brought in a real mug for Simon Legree, or whoever this character is who's coming."

He didn't look at all like Simon Legree. What he reminded Lacey of most was the guy who'd sat in front of her in calculus class senior year of high school. The one who actually enjoyed the class.

Peter Williams was very methodical. He sat at Lacey's desk and requested records, brushing at the lapels of his navy suit once in a while to make sure no dust contaminated it. Next to Jack he looked pale and plain. He wasn't exactly bad looking, Lacey decided. It was just that his quiet, ordinary demeanor couldn't compete well with red suspenders and hazel eyes.

Once he came downstairs and was introduced, Jack tried to say volumes to her as he looked over Peter Williams's ruler-straight part, but Lacey ignored him. This wasn't the time and place to start thinking about Jack as anything but the taxpayer in question. She answered Mr. Williams's questions calmly and efficiently and offered him a cup of coffee.

"Is it decaffeinated?" he asked, looking up.

"No, but the pot upstairs is," Jack said. "Let me go get you some." Lacey almost called out to him that he had forgotten Leona's mug, but she held off. If she called, she'd have to hand it to him, and that would blow her careful concentration.

The mug he brought down was pure Jack. It was ringed with awful alligators and oranges on a tan background, the tourist special. Mr. Williams didn't seem to notice. He took a package of low-calorie sweetener out of his inside pocket, tapped it several times, ripped off a minute corner, and poured exactly half of it into his coffee. That maneuver completed, he crimped down the package, put it away carefully, and went back to his audit.

At one o'clock, Lacey was still answering questions. She was willing her stomach not to talk loudly enough for the field auditor to hear. She could just imagine the look that would cross his bland face if her stomach gurgled.

When Jack rescued her, she felt almost grateful. "So, Mr. Williams, do you eat with your victims?" Jack asked, putting down his tools. "I'm about to call the deli down the block and have them send over sandwiches. What can I get you?"

Williams considered the question. "A salad. Low-calorie dressing on the side. No crackers and a diet soda. And a separate check," he said. Lacey used every ounce of willpower she had not to explode. When she had smoothed every trace of laughter out, she gave Jack her lunch order. He nodded and went in the front to see what Leona wanted. The wink he gave her as he walked through the doorway made her shiver with a thrill she couldn't control, just like always. In her present mood, it also made her want to throw a ledger at him.

Lacey was glad she'd made the decision to quit after the audit. There was no way she could work near Jack without being constantly uncomfortable. Whether or not she felt as if she could trust him, she was still terribly attracted to him. Every wink, every cocky little gesture, just made her ache in ways she'd never dreamed possible until she met him. Leaving was the only alternative.

When lunch came, Lacey excused herself and took hers into the park half a block down. It was just a bit of open space with a couple of benches, but it was better than trying to avoid Jack in the office. And there was no way she could eat in front of the field auditor. She suspected he wouldn't have approved of the way she ate her nutritionally unsound pastrami sandwich anyway. Just for him, though, she threw away the big garlic dill pickle that came with the sandwich and popped a stick of sugar-free mint gum into her mouth after.

When she came back, the work area around the auditor was as tidy as if he'd never eaten lunch. "He went over the top of the desk with a paper towel afterward to make sure he hadn't left any evidence," Jack muttered as he passed Lacey. Just the deep, low sound of his voice in her ear made her whole right side prickle. Why did he continue to do this to her?

Finally Mr. Williams closed up all the folders, stopped asking questions, and punched sets of figures into his laptop for a while as Jack and Lacey sat at either side of the back room in nervous silence. Jack at least pretended to work on an order for a client. Lacey just sat rearranging a pile of paper clips.

After a bit Mr. Williams stopped, checked everything, and punched some commands into the computer. A moment later, the small printer attached hummed, then spat out a sheet of paper. "Well, this looks encouraging," he said, as Lacey tried to relax her shoulders for the first time in hours. Jack seemed to be stretching a kink out of the back of his neck.

Mr. Williams droned on about the financial condition of Dalton's Jewelry for a while. He didn't tell Lacey anything new. She couldn't quite suppress a smile when he painstakingly explained to Jack that he was making just the right move in getting rid of the regular lines and concentrating on the custom business. It was all she could do to keep from grinning.

"Even though you seem to be alleviating your problems of the past, there's still the issue of underreported gains for the year in question," Mr. Williams said. "This is my estimate of what you owe in additional taxes and interest."

He pushed the printed worksheet over to Jack, who looked at it and then looked again. "That's it?"

"I suspect it will be. Of course, someone at the office will be going over all of this information again, and we'll be issuing a full report at a later date," he said. "But this should be a good estimate."

Jack actually grinned. "That's something I could live with. I had visions of it being a lot worse."

"You've obviously had competent financial help, Mr. Dalton." The auditor turned to Lacey. "I trust if I need to have any more information I can call you to get it, Ms. Robbins?"

If she hadn't known better, Lacey would have sworn there was a speculative gleam in the man's eye. Of course, what would come closer to exciting him than a neat and tidy set of ledgers? She stifled a smile. "Let me give you my business card, Mr. Williams. I'm only here on an as-needed basis."

There was no need to worry about this guy calling her on anything but business, Lacey decided. Once he'd talked to any of the kids on the phone, with Becca's music, the video games, and the cat all competing for attention in the background, he'd keep the questions to basic ones about inventory on hand.

Peter Williams took her card and slipped it into a compartmentalized container that he slid into his frighteningly neat briefcase. He shut down his computer, dismantled it, slid it into its case as well, and stood up. He shook hands with both of them, and Jack walked him to the door.

A moment later, Jack was back, clearing the threshold to the back room with a whoop. "That's the first time I ever shook hands with a dead fish. Or at least that's what it felt like." He drummed out a little tune on the desk. "He's done, Lacey. It's over, and I still have a roof over my head. Let's go celebrate."

"No, Jack…," she began.

"Come on. As a grateful client who expected to lose his shirt and is scraping by only losing a few vest buttons, I want to take you out somewhere. I promised a return trip to La Venezia, remember?"

"I know, but—" Lacey seemed unable to finish any of her sentences.

"We'll take Leona with us to chaperone if you want," Jack said, taking hold of Lacey's hands. "Come on, don't say no."

"Jack, you do realize you're still going to have to pay penalties, don't you?" Lacey slipped her hands out of his and reached for the worksheet Williams had left on her desk. "This isn't exactly chicken feed."

Jack looked at the paper and nodded. "But it could have been a whole lot worse. Lacey, even after setting up the trust for Kenton, Jamie's part of the business still had a little left over. A thriving store is what he would have wanted to see, regardless of what we were selling. This way I can pay off the IRS and split what's left between the business and the trust." He did a little dance step around the desk. It was Latin and smooth and compelling. Lacey had to turn her head.

"Come on, I really feel like celebrating," Jack urged.

Leona even agreed to his scheme. The look Lacey shot her had no effect at all. "Help me close up so I can get my purse and go. Harve's out with an old buddy fishing for the day. They'll stop at some awful greasy spoon somewhere once they get done, so I've got no excuse to say no."

"No excuse except my self-respect," Lacey muttered under her breath. Other than her determination not to be with Jack anywhere but the shop, Lacey didn't have any reason not to go either. The kids knew this was going to be a rough day, and she'd left Becca money to order a pizza in. Nobody would complain if she was late.

Maybe she was supposed to do this, she reasoned with herself. Perhaps this was what she needed to say good-bye to Jack, to put some closure on their relationship. She kept telling herself that as she combed her hair and fixed her lipstick with shaky fingers.

Nineteen

This time Lacey didn't fidget while she waited for her appetizer. For once she felt like her audit skills had earned her dinner at the expensive restaurant. She enjoyed the plump pink shrimp with remoulade sauce, not even protesting when Jack swiped one. She was just thankful his hand didn't brush hers when he filched it off her plate.

"If you want more, you can have them," she told him.

"No, one will do," he said with an engaging grin. "Besides, I don't want you going hungry. No sense adding another grievance against me to your long list."

"Sarcasm doesn't become you, Jack," Lacey said softly.

"Excuse me," Jack said. "I just wanted tonight to turn out differently."

"Am I in the way?" Leona asked, her eyebrows lifting almost up to her silvered hairline.

"No, you're not," Lacey and Jack both chorused at once.

They had to laugh at that.

"Let's call a truce then for dinner, all right? A truce among friends and former coworkers," Lacey said for emphasis.

"If that's the best I can hope for, I'll take it. But don't be surprised if I try for more."

"Nothing you could do would surprise me, Jack." Lacey broke off another piece of the French bread and buttered it.

There was an awkward lull in the conversation for a few minutes. None of them seemed to know quite how to fill it. Lacey had a sip of water, the lemon slice floating delicately in a feathery little circle.

"Leona, I keep forgetting to ask you something," Lacey said.

"You mentioned a lady in your Bible study a while back who does house-sitting. Does she also sit for houses that have people in them?"

"Jan Phillips? I think so. Since she retired from her full-time job, she's really enjoyed all the little part-time things. Especially since Bill's gone," Leona said. "I'll ask her if you want."

"Please," Lacey said. "I'm going to parents' weekend at Brooke's college in Atlanta in about ten days, and I haven't found anybody to stay with the kids. It really just hit me last night that I don't have Brooke to rely on for that anymore." She sipped some more of her water and wrinkled her nose. "Of course, Becca is trying to convince me that she could be the woman of the house just fine, but not even in my nightmares would I agree."

Leona nodded. "I can understand that. I'll call Jan when I get home tonight. Can I give her your phone number if she's interested?"

"Yes, thanks," Lacey said. It was a relief when the main course came and there was a reason for the silence at the table.

The veal on her plate was tender and well seasoned, but it might as well have been liver for all the enthusiasm Lacey felt toward her meal. Amid the relief that this was the last full day she would have to spend with Jack was a growing dread…for the same reason.

Pushing her vegetables around on the plate, Lacey told herself she shouldn't feel torn. He was irresponsible and unreliable. Also totally gorgeous and the most appealing guy she'd met in years. The fact that the kids really liked him and even Britt didn't seem to harbor any ill feelings shouldn't cloud her judgment any. Jack Dalton was just not to be trusted.

Still, she was wrestling with her decision to quit the job and to stop seeing Jack. If she had a strong, positive feeling that this was what God wanted her to do, walking away would still be painful, but comforting in a way too. As it was, it was just painful.

Lacey gave up on eating and put down her fork. "That dessert trolley is going to have to pass me by again," she said with a sigh. Tonight chocolate-mousse cake would taste like sawdust.

Leona scooted her chair back from the table. "I'm with Lacey. This place is bad for my figure." She grinned at Jack, sitting next to her. "And I'm so glad you took us here. Thanks, kiddo." She stood up and settled her handbag on her arm. "Well, even Harve should be heading home by now. With luck he's even got the fish cleaned. Thank you again, Jack, for dinner, and, Lacey, I'll call Jan tonight."

They thanked her in unison and watched as Leona strolled out of the restaurant into the twilight. "She's a great lady," Lacey said.

"Sure is. I'm glad she's so excited about the new turn the business is taking. I'll need all the help I can get."

"Don't start sounding pathetic on me, Jack," Lacey said, feeling her hackles rise. "I've made my decision, and I'm sticking to it. We're both better off each going our own way. If I stay I'll just get dependent on you again and then—"

"And then you're positive I'll let you down, is that it?"

Lacey nodded, looking down at the tablecloth. It was too hard to look up at Jack, knowing from the sound of his voice that there would be deep gold fire glinting in his eyes. "Lacey, how many times have I let you down? Once."

"Once is enough," Lacey said, playing with her napkin to keep her hands busy. "I need somebody stable in my life right now, Jack. Somebody I can depend on."

"At least give me a chance to show you that I'm not going to do it again."

"Don't, Jack. Please." It took all of Lacey's control not to let the tears well up.

"Okay." He reached for the bill and scanned it, then paid it while Lacey sat silently. She started to rise to make some attempt at thanks so she could leave before he walked her across the street. "Don't go. There's something at the shop you need to see."

Lacey didn't argue. It would take more energy than she had to waste right now. The drive home was going to be hard enough, even though it was only a few miles. She didn't need to fuel her anxiety with another argument with Jack.

The bell clanged softly when he unlocked the door. Inside the shop, he switched a light on in the back room and motioned for her to come in, past the doorway dividing the shop and the workroom. He turned his back to her and fumbled with a small box on the table. "This is yours." He handed it to her over her protests. "It's not from me. A client called and commissioned it. It was supposed to be for your birthday next month, but I probably won't see you then. So take it now. She won't mind."

Lacey opened the box. In it an enameled pin was perched on the velvet. It was a butterfly, perfect and iridescent, with glowing wings. She gasped at the beauty of it, nestling it in her hand. "Brooke," she said in a whisper.

"Yeah. She called me one day last week. I'd really like to meet her sometime, Lacey." He took the pin out of the box and gently pinned it to the front of her jacket. "It looks good on you. She was right about the colors."

His fingers brushed her cheek gently while pinning the butterfly to her lapel, and Lacey finally lost the control she'd been holding over her emotions. One tear slid down her cheek, then another, before she could stop.

"Aw, Lacey." Jack's broad thumb was warm and rough on her skin as he dried her tears. "Don't do that. Or if you do, stay so I can try to make it all better."

His voice was steady, but the look behind his dark eyes was one of pleading. Lacey shook her head. "You can't make it all better, Jack. No matter how long I stay."

"Can't or won't—because you don't trust me?" Jack's voice had an edge to it. "At least cut me some slack, Lacey. I'm not as irresponsible as you think."

"No? Then how could you forget a child's birthday when you were all she wanted?"

"You know I didn't forget. And she survived." Jack sounded tired, and when Lacey looked at him, even through the blur of tears he seemed slumped, almost defeated. "Maybe that's the point. I'm tired of being all anybody wants. I spent years trying to do it all with Jamie, and it didn't work, Lacey. He's still just as dead as if I hadn't done anything. So maybe I don't want to get in the position of being all anybody ever wants again."

"Not even for me?" Lacey wondered where she found the courage for the words. "I'm not Jamie."

"You are most definitely not Jamie. And what you want is probably a thousand times more dangerous. You have a life I can only dream of right now. It looks good from the outside, Lacey, but it scares me silly. I just can't make that kind of sacrifice." He touched the butterfly pin, and it shimmered. Then Lacey looked up into Jack's eyes, and the shimmering light she saw there was brighter than the reflection off the pin...and much more intense.

"This isn't solving anything, Jack. I don't think it ever will."

Lacey's voice was choked. She had to leave, or spend the night getting deeper into something that wasn't going anywhere. "I have to go now. Good-bye, Jack." The bell above the shop door drowned out whatever reply he made.

At home, once the kids were all settled in their rooms, she called Brooke. Lying on the bed, talking to her, telling her everything that had happened, Lacey reached for a corner of the sheet. Naturally somebody had raided the box of tissues by the bed, and it was empty. She talked and dabbed with the sheet corner, which got wetter and wetter.

"I'm glad you liked the butterfly anyway," Brooke said. "I just finished a class in self-defense for women. You want me to come home and beat this character up for you?"

She would, too. Lacey choked out a laugh at the thought of Brooke, tall and dark-haired and formidable in anger. "No thanks, sweetie. I do appreciate the offer, but it wouldn't solve any problems." She dried her tears and listened to Brooke's stories of life on campus. When she found herself almost drifting off while she listened, she broke in.

"I need to turn out the light here before I fall asleep on you."

Brooke hooted. "Remember the time Becca ran up a twenty-dollar phone call to Illinois when she fell asleep talking long distance?"

"All too well," Lacey replied. "Talk to you later, okay?"

"Okay. Promise me you'll pray about this a lot. And hang in there," Brooke said with intensity.

Lacey put the phone back in its cradle and sighed. She'd hang in there, all right. Only this time it was going to take all ten fingernails.

~ ~ ~ ~ ~

Leona's Bible study partner Jan Phillips was solid. It was the only word Lacey could think of to describe her. Her iron gray hair was cut in a short, sensible style, and everything she wore could probably drip dry. She had broad, square hands that looked like they were used to keeping busy, and she carried a small notebook all during her interview and jotted things down in it.

Oops took instant offense to her for some reason and went to hide under the sofa. But no one else seemed to be horrified during Jan's brief visit to interview. Becca, complete with head-phones, probably wouldn't have noticed if the lady had three eyes, Lacey decided. But Jan definitely noticed Becca.

"Does she have a limit on how many hours a day she can wear those things?"

Lacey shook her head. "It's never been a problem."

Mrs. Phillips jotted something in her notebook. "And she gets home from school when? Has what chores? And are there any allergies I should know about?"

"Three o'clock, loads the dishwasher every third day, helps cook dinner, keeps her room clean, and is allergic to nothing but detests most cooked green vegetables."

Lacey gave the same rundown on Brian and Britt. By the time she was done, there were several notebook pages full, and Mrs. Phillips clucked. "I can see that meal planning is going to be a challenge to make sure everybody gets all their nutrients around here." She narrowed her eyes suspiciously. "Do they take vitamins?"

"Not usually," Lacey admitted weakly. She wasn't going to get any parenting gold stars from this lady.

After she'd told her everything she could think of and then some about the kids, she offered Mrs. Phillips a glass of iced tea

189

and settled her in a kitchen chair. "So tell me a little bit about yourself," Lacey said.

"Not much to tell, really," Mrs. Phillips said, smoothing out an infinitesimal wrinkle in the place mat in front of her. "I'm sure Leona told you I do this on a regular basis. I don't have too many hobbies, unless you count crossword puzzles and game shows." She took a sip of tea. "Now if you limit the kids' television time, I can always tape them and watch those after they're in bed."

"That won't be necessary," Lacey assured her.

"Good. I do hate to miss my shows," Mrs. Phillips said. It was the first hint of real enthusiasm for anything except dietary fiber that Lacey had seen. Maybe she was human after all.

By the time Mrs. Phillips was ready to leave, they'd settled on a time for her to come over on the following Thursday and Lacey had promised that the house would be clean and fully stocked with groceries. "And I'll be back Sunday afternoon by three, unless we get stuck in Atlanta for some reason," she said.

Mrs. Phillips reached into her purse and pulled out a packet of forms. "Almost forgot these. The top one is twenty-four-hour emergency information on where to reach you and at least one other responsible adult, and the bottom is a hospital permission slip in case anything unfortunate happens." Giving them to Lacey, she waved almost cheerfully and headed for the shiny compact car parked precisely in the center of the driveway.

Lacey closed the door, reading the forms. A second responsible adult? Brooke was a little far away to count. Automatically she thought of Jack. He was at least an adult and he did know the kids. She went to the kitchen to rummage in the junk drawer for a pencil to try to complete Mrs. Phillips's forms.

Trying to get her tax customers squared away for the season and getting the house and kids ready for her trip took all of

Lacey's time for a week. She kept meaning to call Jack and tell him she had used his name on the form, but she kept putting it off.

The night before her trip she called Jack. They hadn't talked since he delivered her last paycheck from the store, over a week before. Then it had been awkward, him standing outside the door, her steadfastly determined not to invite him in. Tonight on the phone it wasn't much better. "I thought I ought to tell you I used your name," she said, describing the forms from Mrs. Phillips.

"You put me down as a responsible adult? Gee, Lacey, you must have been desperate."

Lacey could feel the edge of pain in his voice. "Jack, I don't want to get into that argument now, okay? I wouldn't put anybody's name down for something that important without telling them. All right?"

"All right. I'm sorry, Lacey. I guess I just don't like it much around here anymore without you. Get some rest before your trip, okay?"

"I'll try." Lacey leaned against the kitchen wall, leaning with her forehead on the cool tile after she hung up. It was a good thing she was so busy. Otherwise she would have time to think about how much it hurt to talk to Jack, even on the phone. As it was, she had to pack and do two loads of laundry before midnight. It was going to be a tight race.

By the time Mrs. Phillips rang the bell on Thursday morning, ten minutes earlier than promised, the forms were filled out. Lacey had really had to scavenge to come up with some of the information. What this woman was going to do with the kids' blood types, she had no idea. "Now I've put down work and home numbers here for another adult, Jack Dalton. He's Leona's boss, and he knows the kids. If anything should come

191

up that you don't feel is worth bothering me for, feel free to call him," Lacey said. *He may not be any help,* she added to herself, *but at least the form doesn't have any blank spaces.*

The drive to the airport was uneventful. Lacey remembered the last time she had been here, to take Brooke. She looked down at the gleaming little butterfly on her lapel. So much had happened since then. And now everything was back to the same old story. She had really tried to be a fun person, to seek those adventures. With Jack around, it had almost seemed to work. But with Jack around, there were dimensions to life she wasn't sure she could handle.

If she was honest with herself, she had to admit that distrust wasn't the only reason she'd walked away from Jack. Fear was the other one. With Jack around, Lacey had to let go of the tight routine she had made for herself. She had to let herself feel all the emotions, including those of being trapped into raising kids that weren't hers. And she had to admit that deep inside were still bits of the rebellious, rowdy person she had been at fifteen. If she walked away now, she could just be Lacey Robbins, cool, collected accountant and surrogate parent. She could forget all those other emotions that scared her to death.

Surely it was better this way, she told herself as she settled into her seat on the plane and fastened her safety belt. She reached into her carry-on bag and pulled out a book. It was going to be a very long flight.

Twenty

God was flexing his humor muscles. That was the only way Lacey could explain her flight to Atlanta. It was calm, peaceful, and the perfect atmosphere for her to read the book she had brought along. There were no squalling babies or teenagers with Walkmen plugged in at max volume sitting next to her. The only distraction, if you could even call it that, was the adorable two or three-year-old in the next row. And she was being a wonderful traveler.

So why wasn't Lacey relaxed, her shoes kicked off, and twenty pages into her novel? Because the book she picked up in the airport gift shop was one she'd read already in hardcover. The new cover on the paperback fooled her, but only through page three. Lacey put it back in her purse.

So what else was there to do? She could think and pray. She needed to do that, to sort out this mess with Jack Dalton in her mind. And she really did have another book with her. In the side zip pocket of her purse was her emergency Bible. Bright orange to foil her losing it and not much bigger than a deck of cards, it was always there.

"Okay, Lord," she muttered, picking it up. "This was obviously your idea. Where am I supposed to go from here?" She stroked the soft leather cover and riffled the pages. The tiny print would probably give her a headache. Air travel usually did anyway, so it wasn't a loss. At least this way it would be a productive headache, she told herself.

It was hard to keep her mind on her reading somehow. Lacey could feel herself in the gaze of some other individual. Looking up, she could see the head of the passenger in front of her, up to a button nose. She had a mop of pale yellow curls, and huge blue eyes. She reminded Lacey a little of Britt at the same age, with that "what can I do now?" expression that inquisitive children of a certain age always hold.

"Hi," Lacey said, wondering if this child was old enough to know not to talk to a stranger.

"Hi," she answered back. "I'm Piper. What's your name?"

"I'm Lacey," she told the child. "She's not bothering me, really," she said to the mother, who had leaned around the seat to make sure the child standing in her own seat wasn't aggravating a stranger. "I'm having a good time."

"Okay," the young woman said, sounding tired. "If she gets to be a nuisance, let me know."

"I will," Lacey promised her, wondering how this one could ever be a nuisance. "So how old are you, Piper?"

"Free," she said, holding up the requisite number of fingers. "And I gots money!"

"Oh, my. Lots of money?" Lacey asked her. Piper nodded vigorously, making her curls bounce.

"Lots of money," she echoed. Her head disappeared for a moment, then popped back up. "It was in my pocket," she said, reaching a clenched fist over the seat. Lacey could see the dimpled indentations on each knuckle, sweet reminders of Piper's disappearing babyhood.

Piper opened her hand over Lacey's lap, letting loose a cascade of pennies. "See? Lots of money," she said.

"You certainly do have lots of money," Lacey said, picking up the pennies. "Seven cents."

"How many dollars?" Piper asked.

"None yet, not right here, but plenty of pennies." Lacey gathered them up and held them out in an open palm. "Do you want them back."

"Yes, please. Can I come get them?" Piper leaned over to her invisible mother. "Let me out so I can get my moneys," she told her.

The mother's head appeared around the seat again. "Are you sure this is all right? I don't usually let her wander, especially on airplanes."

"It's fine with me," Lacey said, enchanted by the child. "Come on, Piper, come get your moneys."

Piper wriggled across her mother's lap. Tiny tennis shoes slithered into the aisle first, then overall-clad legs and sturdy tanned arms in a short-sleeved white T-shirt. In an instant she was scrambling up Lacey's lap. "A book. Are there stories in it?"

"Lots of stories. No pictures, just the kind you have to make yourself in your own head. But plenty of stories."

"Good." Piper settled herself comfortably in Lacey's lap. "Give me back my moneys, please. Then read me a story from your book. About moneys."

"About moneys," Lacey echoed, wondering where to go with this one. As she transferred the pennies to Piper, who put them carefully in the front bib pocket of her overalls, she thought about that one. "This book doesn't say a lot about moneys, Piper. It says a lot about Jesus. Do you know Jesus?"

Piper, nodding until her curls bounced again, launched into a rousing version of "Jesus Loves Me." Lacey nodded along with her. "That's right, Piper. Jesus does love you. And this book is that Bible the song talks about. But it doesn't say much about moneys. More about love." She got a sudden inspiration and turned farther into the book of Matthew than she had been reading earlier. "It does say something about pennies in here, though. I remember that." Looking quickly down the page, she found it. No sense reading about Pharisees to a three-year-old, but the moneys part she could understand.

"Do you know what a sparrow is?" Piper shook her head, moving the curls in a new direction. "Well, it's a little bitty bird. So small that you could probably even hold one in your hand. And Jesus says here that people could buy two of them for a penny. And you know what else?"

"What?"

Lacey ached for the sweetness in that trusting expression. "He says that God knows about every one of those birds, even the ones that are two for a penny, and not one of them will fall out of the sky without him knowing about it. Not one."

"Not one," Piper echoed.

"And he loves us even more than the birds and cares about everything we're doing. Lots more than the birds."

"Lots more," Piper said, and somewhere in her expression Lacey caught an echo of Kenton and his question about the size of God. *"Huge. Humongous,"* she could hear him saying in her mind. With that, something hit her with the strength of the plane they were riding in.

Sparrows are two for a penny, Lacey, a small voice seemed to whisper. *And I care about them and take care of them. Myself.* Lacey leaned back into her seat, her head spinning. Piper seemed to sense that Lacey needed some time by herself. Or maybe the child had just hit the end of her attention span. "I need to go see Mom," she told Lacey, sliding off her lap. "Bye."

"Bye," Lacey said absently, watching Piper clamber onto the seat in front of her. Even there she could hear Piper chattering to her mother, but she couldn't make out the words. There were too many things swirling in her mind.

Children, one with a handful of pennies, and one with empty hands. Both were pointing her to what God wanted her to see. That he loved them all personally and would take care of them all. And he would do it in his own time and in his own way. "Oh, Father," Lacey whispered. "Please, please forgive me. I've been so busy trying to run Jack's life and make him see what I thought was your plan for him that I never let him talk to you and find that plan for himself. Please, Lord, help me to release him so he can do just that."

Lacey's eyes were swimming with tears. When she blinked, they cleared a little, and she could focus on the object built into the seat back directly in front of her. It was a telephone. Of course there had been one on every airplane she had flown on in the last couple years. She saw travelers using them once in a while and knew they were prohibitively expensive. Nothing a prudent CPA like herself would ever consider using. However she had to talk to Jack. Now. It wouldn't even wait until she was on the ground in Atlanta in half an hour. She read the instructions on using the silly thing and pulled out her calling card. This time she could almost hear God laughing out loud.

When the phone rang at Dalton's, Jack jumped. Deep into his design project, he hadn't expected any interruptions. Not that he was really designing anything. Rather he was drifting in his mind again, wondering how to ease the ache he felt over missing Lacey. He missed her every day.

He missed more than just Lacey. If Jack was honest with himself, he had to admit that he missed the kids, the cat, the whole picture. And he missed more than just that. What he missed most of all was Lacey's faith.

Being around Lacey every day, Jack had watched her trust her life to Jesus. All her decisions were made with God's guidance. She walked with him every day in a way Jack found so incredibly different from his own life. Since Jamie's death, God had been such a distant figure. He yearned for the kind of relationship Lacey had with God. Several times he had been on the brink of asking her to show him just how to get there himself. But now she was gone, and there was no one else to ask.

When the phone rang at his elbow, Jack grabbed it like a lifeline. It was never Lacey when it rang, but maybe this time it would be. When he heard her voice, he nearly dropped the receiver in surprise.

"Lacey? I thought you were supposed to be on your way to Atlanta," he said.

Her laugh was shaky. "I am. I'm calling from somewhere over Georgia."

His thoughts were spinning. "Wow, Lacey, what's wrong with the plane? I can't imagine anything short of an imminent plane crash making you spend that kind of money on a phone call to me." In his heart, Jack prayed that nothing of the kind was happening, even as the cynical words left his lips.

"The plane's fine," Lacey told him. "But I'm a wreck. I've got a new friend, and she just showed me something I should have seen for myself weeks ago."

"Oh?" Jack tried to remember to breathe while he listened to Lacey.

Her words tumbled out fast. "Oh, Jack, I've been so silly. I feel like the Queen of Stubborn here. All this time I've been after you and after you—'do it my way' about everything. Will you ever forgive me?"

"In an instant if I thought you needed forgiveness, Lacey, but I still don't get it," Jack told her.

"I started out all right, Jack. I was trusting Jesus in everything, and so I just figured that he was showing me what he wanted for you…that I was supposed to show it to you. But that's all wrong."

198

"It is?" Jack felt stunned. "But, Lacey, I want what you have. If you could just show me how to get it, I'd be the happiest man in the world."

"No, you wouldn't. Not any more than I'm the happiest woman." Her voice was filled with emotion, even five hundred miles away. "I can do something else that will do us both a lot more good."

"What's that?" Jack wasn't sure he wanted to hear the answer.

"I can let you go," she said.

"No, Lacey. You've already done that. And it isn't working. I miss you terribly—"

Lacey broke into his argument. "I don't mean walk away from you, Jack. That's what I did, and you're right, it isn't working. What I need to do is release you. Stop running your life and turn my concerns for you over to God. You and Jesus need to sort this out directly, and I need to let you do just that."

"I can't do that," Jack argued. "Not without you. I don't have that kind of faith, Lacey."

"Oh, come on, Jack. You do. Anybody does, if they just ask for it. Do you think that I was this perfect person when Beth and Kevin died? That I just said, 'Okay, fine, God, this is just great, whatever you want'? Of course not. I screamed and ranted and cried and lost it. But I kept asking God for his peace, too. And when I was really asking for it, it came."

"And that's what I need to do? Ask for peace?" Jack asked, feeling incredibly dense.

"I don't know what you need to ask for, Jackson," Lacey's soft, sure voice came over the line. "But I know that you need to ask Jesus for whatever it is personally, and I need to get out of your way and stop managing your life."

"Does that mean I won't see you again?"

Lacey answered quickly, as if she could hear the pain in his voice. "On the contrary. It means that once I get back from Atlanta Sunday night, we're going to have to see a lot of each other. Because I have the feeling I messed up big time walking away from you and Dalton's Jewelry. It just means I can't be some kind of conduit between you and God, Jack. That's not the way things work."

"But your walk with Jesus seems so…personal, Lacey," Jack said, stumbling. "How can I ever do that?"

"Just ask, Jack. Just reach out your heart and your hands and ask. God has so much waiting for you. I know it." Lacey was silent for a minute. "And there's somebody waiting for me right now. It seems I have to hang up now so we can land. I love you."

"I love you too, Lacey," Jack said, putting the phone back in its cradle. He sat silent for a moment, feeling more alone than he had felt in his entire life and knowing that whether or not he kept that feeling was entirely his decision.

"I can't stand the silence, God," he prayed out loud. "I know you have a plan for my life. I sit in church every Sunday and wonder why you don't show me what it is. I've watched Lacey for months, envying her because she seemed to know you. Please show me the way. Let me be all yours."

Jack sat quiet, drained. He was so tired. There were tears too close to the surface for his comfort, closer than they had been in all the months since Jamie died. But with those tears was an incredible peace. In this short span of time, he had stopped feeling alone.

The phone rang again. He was tempted to let Leona get it. She must have been busy, though, because it rang again, twice, and he finally picked it up. "Dalton's Jewelry," he said, trying to keep his voice steady for the benefit of the unknown customer on the other end.

"Jack?" Kimberly's voice sounded strained. "Thank God I got ahold of you. I need to ask you a terribly big favor, and you can't say no."

There was no anger welling up in response to her statement, Jack discovered. *This one's all yours, Lord,* he found himself thinking silently. When he answered Kimberly out loud, he didn't have to put any effort into steadying his voice. It was solid and firm. "Sure, Kimberly. Whatever it takes. Tell me."

Lacey rented a car and drove out to Brooke's college dorm. Brooke was waiting for her, finished with classes for the day and ready to go have a cappuccino and get Lacey settled in a nearby hotel.

"So when did you start drinking coffee?" Lacey asked her niece as they sipped their coffee at the student union. At least that's what Lacey would have called it from her college days. It looked more like a food court actually, with a bookstore thrown in.

"When it's cold out, I switch from diet cola over to this. More sophisticated, I guess." Brooke wrinkled her nose, laughing at herself. "Of course with the milk and chocolate syrup I usually get in it, it's just hot cocoa with a charge. Some sophistication. So tell me what's going on. I expected to be offering you tea and sympathy after our phone call the other night. What happened?"

It was odd seeing Brooke act all grown up sometimes, Lacey reflected. Sort of like having a baby Beth to talk to. The young woman had her mother's wisdom and intuition in a young body. "Well, it's a long story. We may need a second cup of this stuff," Lacey began and launched in on pennies and Piper and the whole jumbled mess, knowing that Brooke would be the one person who would understand it all.

It did take a second cup of coffee. Lacey made sure hers was decaffeinated so there was some chance of her sleeping before Friday. By the time Lacey was finished, Brooke was leaning back in her chair, smiling like a Cheshire cat. "Wow, Aunt Lacey. That is heavy stuff," she said. "Real adventure this time, huh?"

"What do you mean?" Lacey stirred around the dregs in her cup.

"When you told me about this seeking adventure stuff, I kept waiting for this to happen. For the Lord to throw a real challenge at you and see what happened. Now it sounds like he really has. What do you think will happen now?"

Lacey smiled and held both hands palm up. "That's the crazy part. I don't have the faintest idea. But I'm pretty sure you're right about the challenge part. With your brother and sisters involved, let's hope I'm strong enough to stand whatever the Lord stirs up." They laughed together, and Lacey started picking up the extra napkins on the table, ready to clean up and go find her hotel room. Suddenly she felt like taking a quick nap before going anywhere else with Brooke. And for a change she had no worries that would keep her from sleeping like a baby.

Twenty-One

I want my mama," Kenton wailed, splayed out like a pile of laundry on the floor of Jack's apartment.

"So do I," Jack muttered, watching him with a helpless feeling. "I want my mama too."

Kenton looked up. "You've got a mama?" This was intriguing news, coming from a man he obviously thought of as older than dirt.

"Yep, Kenton, I've got a mama. And right about now I want her too," Jack told him. He had no idea what he was going to do with a two-year-old boy for three or four days. This was going to take a lot of prayer.

His head was spinning. Was this how Lacey had felt when her sister died, leaving her in charge of the kids? At least Kimberly would be back in a few days, once she recovered from the emergency appendectomy she was probably undergoing right this minute. And there was only one of Kenton.

Of course, at this age one was enough. Kenton was done crying for a while, but he was still sprawled out on Jack's floor. "You got any toys? Or cartoons? Or any juice?"

"Let's see. I've got colored pencils. Probably too mature for you. No cartoons because I don't have a TV. And I've got orange juice, I think."

"No apple juice?" Kenton asked incredulously. What kind of place is this? his tone of voice seemed to say.

"No apple juice. Sorry, buddy," Jack told him. "Want to go get some with me? We can pick up a few other things you like."

"Sure," Kenton said, springing up off the floor. "Can we get candy?"

"Not much," Jack told him. He knew that Kimberly did not believe that candy was part of the staple diet of a growing child. He also figured that Kenton was going to try to push the envelope here while he had the chance. "But maybe a little bit."

"Okay!" Kenton crowed. Before Jack could put a jacket on the squirmy little body, the phone rang again. He went for it, hoping that maybe it was the hospital. Maybe they had made a big mistake and Kimberly didn't really need her appendix out after all. Maybe Kenton could go home tonight.

"Hello. Jack Dalton speaking," he said into the phone.

"Jack?" It was Becca. But she didn't sound like the flip, confident young woman that she normally was on the phone and in person. "We've got a problem. A big one."

And I can help solve it? Jack asked silently. He took a deep breath while trying to ease Kenton into his jacket. "What's the matter, Becca?"

Her voice was shaky. "Could you come stay with us? See, Mrs. Phillips called home to check on her messages, and there was this really strange message on her machine about being a fill-in contestant on a big game show, but she has to go, like, tonight. And she can't reach Aunt Lacey for some reason, and she really wants to go, and I don't really want to be in charge, and—"

"Sure, Becca," Jack told her. "Let me put a few things in a suitcase, and I'll be over. Put Mrs. Phillips on the phone." He had to be certifiably insane. But at the same time, the kids could probably help with Kenton.

He squared things with Mrs. Phillips, hung up, and tried to finish putting Kenton's jacket on. "Little change of plans, Kenton. We're going to go play with some big kids. And I know they have apple juice. And a TV."

"All right," Kenton said. Then a pained look crossed his face. "I gotta go."

"So, go," Jack said, unaware of why he had to be informed of this decision.

Kenton's consternation increased. "I gotta go. And I can't do my overalls." Or his jacket apparently.

"Now I really want my mom," Jack told him, trying to complete the undressing before an accident happened. In his mind he was already forming the phone call to Thea Dalton. It was time to call for reinforcements. He was close to laughter and tears at the same time. Only God could have led him where he was right now. And only God could give him the strength to see this through.

Lacey flopped onto the bed in her hotel room, feeling worn out again. Brooke sure knew how to cram a week's worth of activities into a day. It almost kept her from missing the kids. And Jack.

There was no use pretending anymore that she didn't miss him terribly. She wondered what had gone on in his life in the last two days. Some inner sense told her that it was exciting and wonderful, and she itched to find out what it was.

Lacey's hands shook as she dialed Jack's number. Why was she holding her breath as she waited for him to answer? She let it out slowly and kept counting the rings. When they reached ten, she dialed the workshop. No answer there either. She put the phone down gently on the cradle.

She had to talk to somebody. Her call home last night had been extremely brief. She'd gotten her timing all wrong, and Mrs. Phillips had been putting Britt to bed, or so Brian had said, and he and Becca had been too busy squabbling over something to really talk.

Tonight there was no answer at all. Lacey wondered if Brian had been able to charm Mrs. Phillips into breaking the nutritional barriers and going out for ice cream. It sounded like a good idea. Too bad room service couldn't deliver a fudge-swirl cone.

By Saturday night, Lacey was almost desperate to call home and talk to a real, live person. After another full day of parents'-weekend things with Brooke, they separated to shower and change for dinner. Lacey laid full length on the bed and kicked off her shoes. Pumps had to be the most lethal instrument of torture ever invented. "C'mon, somebody pick up the phone," she muttered. On the fourth ring, Brittany finally answered. "Hi, sweetie, it's Aunt Lacey."

"Hi. We're going to have pizza for dinner."

"That sounds pretty good," Lacey said, smiling. She was surprised the kids had talked Mrs. Phillips into pizza. But after all, it was nutritionally balanced. That was always Becca's argument anyway.

They chatted for a few minutes, and Lacey switched the phone to her other ear, stretching luxuriously on the bed. "Let me talk to Becca, okay?"

"Uh, she's in the shower," Brittany said in a small voice.

"Well, then, how about Brian?"

There was a pause before she answered. "He's in the shower too."

"Okay, then Mrs. Phillips. I need to tell her what time I'm getting in tomorrow."

"Ummm—she's in the shower too." Her voice was almost a whisper.

"No good, Britt. We only have two showers," Lacey said.

Then the litany finally sank through Lacey's brain, and she sat up fast. "Brittany Kaye, are you home alone?"

"Just for a few minutes. Becca went to a friend's house, and Brian went with Uncle Jack to get the pizza, and—"

"Uncle Jack? Where is Mrs. Phillips?"

"She had to go to California. When she called her answering machine there was a message about being on the $100,000 Jackpot Show and she had to leave. So Becca called Uncle Jack, and he came over. A little kid came with him," Brittany said simply. "Did I eat strange stuff when I was little? Last night at bathtime Kenton ate soap."

"Kenton." Lacey felt a rising sense of panic. "So what are you doing alone in the house?"

"Well, Uncle Jack was going to send Brian for the pizza alone, but then it was raining and he didn't want him to get his cast wet and—"

"His cast?" Lacey shrieked. "He didn't have a cast when I left."

"Oops," Brittany said. "I wasn't supposed to tell that part."

"I'll be back as soon as I can," Lacey said and hung up the phone.

An hour on the phone found Lacey no flights to Orlando until morning. "Okay, Lord, this is obviously your way of telling me to let Jack handle this one. I wouldn't think he was capable or even willing, but that must be between the two of you. Help me accept that and go take Brooke out to dinner."

She wouldn't be able to eat, or sleep, probably, until after she was back on the ground in Orlando and could see all of this for herself and make sure the kids were okay. It was going to be a long twelve or fifteen hours.

It was after ten o'clock Sunday morning before she arrived in front of the house. Amazingly it seemed to be in one piece.

After her conversation with Brittany, Lacey had been sure she'd come back to a few charred cinder blocks and half of a charred palm tree.

Jack's car was in the driveway. It and the pizza box leaning against the garbage can in the garage seemed to be the only things out of place. Lacey opened the door, and the cat came winding around her ankles, nearly tripping her as she shoved her suitcase through the door.

"Move, Oops. I need to get through." It was just too quiet, even for Sunday morning. There were no showers running, no music playing. It nearly stopped Lacey's heart when she considered what new disasters might be promised by the silence. She listened a moment. There was a humming in the silence, and she followed it into the family room.

Lacey was even more confused when she got there than she had been before. A neat, compact woman with hair streaked with silver sat reading a story to a blond toddler. Kenton.

"Hi, I'm Lacey Robbins. I live here. And when I left I had three kids. Where are they?"

The woman smiled and closed the book. "Kenton, let grandma stop for a while, okay? Want to play the game Brian taught you?"

He nodded and slid off her lap, and she turned on the video game. "I'm Thea Dalton. Your kids are upstairs with my kid. I sent them up to roust him out of bed about half an hour ago."

Lacey still stood in the doorway, her head spinning. "Everybody's okay?"

Jack's mother smiled. "I think so. After last night, today's an anticlimax. Why don't we go into the kitchen and have a cup of coffee? Nobody has to know you're home for a few more minutes."

Lacey was too stunned to argue. She followed Thea into the kitchen and sat down at her own kitchen table, watching Thea pour coffee.

"I gather I have you to thank for something," Thea said, setting down the cup and pouring one for herself. "I have a grandson. That still sounds a little strange, but it's wonderful." Her face clouded over for a minute. "My husband, John, is out playing handball with his usual partner. It's going to take him a while to digest all of this. He went back home this morning as soon as he could."

Her smile was wry. "I seem to be surrounded by men who take a while to come to terms with problems. I know John. He'll go thwack that ball this morning. And he'll tell his partner all about things. By this afternoon he'll start digesting it all himself, and by tomorrow we'll be at the sporting-goods store looking for something for Kenton."

Lacey still didn't know what to say. "But how—when did Jack call you?"

"He needed reinforcements last night. It seems Kimberly collapsed at work. She was nearly frantic when the doctor wouldn't release her from the hospital, and Jack was the only person she could think of to call."

She shook her head. Lacey could see where Jack got those mischievous, sparkling eyes. His mother's were even a deeper brown mixed in with green, if that was possible. "I think the cast did him in. Don't worry, by the way—it's only a hairline fracture. And they all survived the emergency room. I'm beginning to think Jack is going to be all right." She put down her coffee cup and looked straight at Lacey.

"Don't give up on him. There's a solidity to Jack right now that I haven't seen since he was a child. He hasn't said anything, but I can't see where it could be anything but him finding his way back to the Lord."

"I think you're right," Lacey told her, feeling a skyrocket of joy burst inside her.

Thea smiled. "I think you're helping him discover the way back. And I'm so glad that at least one of my sons is going to get to discover that, even if it hurts." She looked at her watch. "They should have gotten him up by now. Want to go upstairs?"

Lacey nodded. She went up the stairs, listening for noise, wondering what she'd find. There was a large amount of blooping and bleeping going on in her office.

They were all there, Brittany still in her nightgown, Becca in jeans, Brian in sweats missing one sleeve and sporting a bright orange fiberglass cast on his left arm. His right was engaged in working a joystick at the computer. It blooped one more time, and he crowed in triumph. "Beat that, sucker!" he yelled as he rolled backward in the desk chair.

Jack, wearing jeans even more disreputable than Becca's and a growth of beard that told Lacey he hadn't shaved in at least two days, slid off the edge of the desk and edged Brian out of the way. "I think I may be awake enough to do just that." He was the first to become aware of Lacey's presence in the room.

"Well, look there. Everybody say good morning to Aunt Lacey. We didn't expect you back until afternoon, but I'm sure glad to see you," he said, looking relieved and tired as he flashed her a smile before going back to the screen,where he was decimating aliens.

"If I could have gotten a flight last night, I would have been in then," Lacey snapped.

"You would have gotten to see all the fireworks if you'd

come then. Britt told us she'd talked to you. It added considerably to the excitement at dinner."

"See, I told you we shouldn't have left her alone, cretin," Becca said, poking Brian on his good arm.

Jack turned his head slightly. "That's ten. Now." Becca looked resigned, sighed, plopped to the floor, and gave him ten perfectly executed push-ups. Lacey was so surprised that she stood there, speechless.

The screen stopped making noises, and Jack backed up. "I never realized that a hitch in the service would be beneficial in child raising. Only time in my life I regretted not enlisting in the Marines with my best friend. Recalling his stories about boot camp has been helpful this weekend, though." He briefly checked Becca's form on the push-ups. "First ones she's done in two days. Things are looking up." He gave Lacey his full attention for the first time since she had entered the room, and that familiar thrill went through her when he winked. "Welcome home."

Jack pushed back his chair. "Let's go have a cup of my mom's coffee. I need it." His arm around her had a slack quality, as if he was near exhaustion.

Lacey wrapped an arm around him. Now she was home, and it felt right. "Gladly. Let me help you down the stairs."

He nuzzled her neck with an unshaven face. "I'll take all the help I can get."

Twenty-Two

I t was hard for Jack not to cling to Lacey like Britt clung to her stuffed animals. She just looked so good, walking into all the insanity he'd been a part of for the weekend.

Still, he let her settle into her own chair in the kitchen instead of pulling her into his lap. The coffee in his mug steamed comfortingly. His mother shooed Kenton outside to have Brian teach him to shoot baskets, and the kitchen was down to only five occupants, Britt and Becca trying to look nonchalant while they eavesdropped. Jack knew that wouldn't last. People drifted in and out of this kitchen like travelers at Grand Central Station.

Lacey sipped her coffee. "The kids told me Mrs. Phillips just kind of vanished. I can't believe it. When I interviewed her she seemed about as solid as a highway divider."

"Yeah, well, even Leona didn't know how serious she was about her game shows. Leona about flipped when the kids called us as work," Jack took a long pull on his coffee, ignoring the fact that it was near scalding. All the better to try and get him alert. Maybe all of this would make more sense if he could mainline some caffeine.

"When did all this happen, anyway?"

Jack's eyes narrowed a little as he thought. "Thursday afternoon, about two hours after Kimberly called."

Lacey's resolve to stay calm nearly broke. "You mean you've been here nearly the whole time I've been gone?"

"Just about. There was that evening in the emergency room. Nobody was here then," Jack said complacently. "You know, you better be glad I'm good with my hands. Otherwise I could never have altered that permission slip so that I was allowed to sign in for Brian at the hospital, instead of Mrs. Phillips."

"You want to tell me about it all at once, before I lose my nerve?" Lacey asked weakly. Thea at the sink gave a knowing laugh that made Jack wonder which of his and Jamie's similar escapades she was thinking of.

"Oops was on the garage roof," Brittany started helpfully. "I wanted to get the ladder, but Brian said he could just go out my window and get him."

"Out your window?" Lacey managed a squeak. She looked pale.

"Sure. We've done it before, just to sit there," Brittany said before her sister and Jack both dove for her mouth. "Oops. I guess I wasn't supposed to say that. But we have. The screen comes out real easy and on the Fourth of July you can see fireworks all the way to—"

"Brittany!" Jack and Becca chorused.

"Well, you can," she went on, unfazed. "Anyway, Oops was on the roof. Brian went to go get him, but one of the shingles broke, and the cat jumped off the roof, and so did Brian. The cat landed on his feet, though," Brittany said thoughtfully, then brightened. "Just like you said he would, Aunt Lacey."

"Great." Lacey turned to Jack. "Where were you while all this was going on?"

"With my head in the dryer trying to figure out why it wasn't putting out any heat," Jack said. "I still have the bump on the back of my head that proves I came out of there fast when I heard the commotion."

Lacey winced. "Really, I do appreciate it all. It's just that it's so…"

"Chaotic? Unstructured? Unexpected?" Jack smiled a very tired smile. "I'll tell you, lady, I'd rather manage three jewelry stores than this mob any day of the week."

"But you did it anyway, didn't you, Uncle Jack?" Brittany said, jumping up and hugging him fiercely.

"I guess I did," he said, hugging her back. "Go get dressed."

"Sure," Britt said, flashing him a smile before she dashed upstairs barefoot.

"What's this 'Uncle Jack' stuff anyway?" Lacey could feel her eyebrow arching as she asked the question.

Britt paused in midrun. "Well, we couldn't call him Mr. Dalton, and just plain Jack didn't sound right. He said this was the power—the power of what?"

"The power of positive thinking," Jack said dryly. "Dress, Britt."

"Okay, fine." In a second she was gone, Becca following her.

"Awfully positive thinking, don't you think, Uncle Jack?" Lacey's voice sounded cynical.

Jack struggled for an answer, and his mother rescued him. "Hey, at least Kenton's the only one I've got calling me Grandma," Thea said, laughing. "Can't blame him for trying, can you, Lacey?"

Lacey wrinkled her nose and smiled. "I guess not." She seemed about to ask Thea more, but the peace in the kitchen was shattered by the fire-engine wail of a small person.

Brian came in carrying the wounded warrior. "He fell on the driveway," he explained. "I know where the Band-Aids and stuff are, Mrs. Dalton. Want me to help?" They all exited the kitchen, the wailing fading up the stairs.

For a moment, Jack heard the silence echo. It was so unusual that he decided to just enjoy it for a minute before saying anything. "Look, Lacey, I was thrilled to do this, even though it wasn't a bundle of fun. It was a crazy way for the

Lord to throw me together with all of this. When we got off the phone Thursday, I prayed. And I asked him to take all of me and do what he wanted. Boy, did he ever want plenty. And now you can tell me 'I told you so' a few times about my folks. My mom, at least."

Lacey looked serious. "Never. But I am glad you finally told her, whatever the circumstances. How did you ever get up the courage?"

"It had nothing to do with courage," Jack admitted. "By last night, my head hurt from bumping it on the dryer, I had run out of ideas on what to feed anybody, we were knee-deep in laundry, and when we told Kenton his mom wasn't coming home until at least today, he went on a nonstop howl. I couldn't cope anymore. I wanted my mom. It was even worth telling her about Kenton to get her to come over."

"Still, it couldn't have been easy," Lacey said. She seemed to look at him with new respect, a fact that filled Jack with relief. He wondered if she would keep the look when she saw the laundry room.

"It wasn't easy. It was one of the hardest things I ever did. But I put my trust in the Lord, and he worked it out fine. Or at least mostly fine. My dad's still ready to blow a gasket over everything, but he'll come around." Jack sat back in his chair. He needed a whole bunch more of that coffee.

Lacey saw his empty cup and got up to fill it. When she set it down, she stayed behind him and wrapped her arms around him. Her perfume smelled wonderful next to his face as she nuzzled into his cheek, then giggled, muffled against him. "You prickle."

"I bet I do. Is it going to make you move?"

"Not very far."

"Oh?" Jack hoped she would say more, much more.

Lacey's voice was soft, and slow in coming. "Yeah. I've got a confession to make. I guess I didn't really call it quits before just because I couldn't trust you. I couldn't trust myself either, Jack."

His skin tingled where she was running a tentative finger at his hairline. "What do you mean?"

"I've been single, running this show my own way, for a long time. It's orderly and neat the way I run it. And I kind of lost sight of the fact that I'm not supposed to be the one running it at all. God is, and he used you to remind me of that."

"Fool that I am." Jack's throat was dry, and he put down another slug of coffee, still trying to ignore the heat. "You were probably right not to trust me, Lacey. I still don't know why I did all this, except that I couldn't do anything else."

"Don't you see?" She squeezed his neck, nuzzling close to his ear. "You could have done it your way. Or even my way. But instead you took the hardest way out and made that sacrifice you kept telling me you couldn't make." She kissed his ear, then pulled away.

"Hey, you're moving," Jack said accusingly.

"I've got to," she said. "I can't just fling myself into your arms and live happily ever after, can I?"

"If you were me, you'd do that," Jack said, sipping his coffee and rubbing his hand over his chin, relishing her fingers kneading his shoulders. "However, being you, you're going to sit here and give me some kind of lecture about why I didn't call you right away Thursday night. Then you're going to tell me you need lots of time to think about things."

Jack could almost feel her smile. "No, Jackson, for once I'm not going to lecture you. This was murder, letting go and knowing that this was all in God's hands and between the two of you. But it worked. And who am I to question God's way of doing things?"

Jack set down his coffee and took her hands. "So you're not going to throw me out immediately?"

"Well, I'll give you fifteen minutes to finish your coffee. Your mom and I can cook breakfast or brunch or whatever for everybody while you shower. Then you can call the hospital. If Kimberly's going to be released, they'll want her out by noon."

"The ever-practical Lacey Robbins." Jack stood and led her around the table to face him. "But first let me say hello properly before I have to say good-bye." He drew her into his arms and nuzzled her cheek, then possessed her lips in a leisurely, thorough fashion that made him shiver.

Jack felt a sense of awe. He looked at the smiling woman in his arms and slowly slipped the bright red frames down her nose, folded them gently, and put them on the table. "Let me practice once, and then we can call them in."

Lacey walked out to the car with Jack as he was taking his things to the trunk. He looked exhausted as he settled the bags and closed the lid. Now it was her turn to put her arms around him. He came into her arms gratefully, and she decided she liked the heavy feeling of his head sagging into her shoulder in an enveloping hug. Even when his chin began to tickle the sensitive area near her neck, it felt good. "Now you realize this doesn't mean I'm going to be popping into the shop bright and early tomorrow morning, don't you?"

"I hadn't given it much thought one way or another," Jack said. "I'm still trying to get my ears to stop ringing from the volume of music that young woman plays."

Lacey chuckled. "And you thought I was grouchy. Hmmpf.

Anyway, I've got to finish up all my clients' returns, schedules, extensions, and on ad infinitum, and point them toward somebody else for the future. So don't count on seeing me there for a while, okay?"

Jack smiled. "Not even Friday?"

"Why Friday?"

Jack's eyes widened with disbelief. "You're being cute, right?"

"Not to my knowledge."

"Your birthday is Friday, Lacey. And I do not intend to miss it. So if you don't come there, I will come here."

"Let's make it here. We don't usually do much celebrating until a month after, when tax season is over and I can breathe again." Lacey watched as he slipped into the car and settled into the seat.

"Fine. We'll keep it low-key. Maybe by then I will feel like I've caught up on my sleep." Jack's mother got into the car and helped Kenton into his car seat. Jack leaned out the window, and Lacey leaned in a little for one last kiss before he left.

"Kiss me, too?" Kenton asked hopefully.

Lacey smiled and blew a kiss to the little boy. He laughed and grabbed at the imaginary kiss.

Jack backed the car out of the driveway, and Lacey waved as Kenton blew a stream of kisses her way. Jack winked and blew one of his own.

Beth used to tell her to be careful what she asked for because she might get it, Lacey reflected as she carried a basket of fresh-smelling towels up to the bathroom. Beth had gotten what she'd asked for, every bit of it. Lacey could still remember her, tanned and golden, holding hands with Kevin that last night before she left with him on their last trip, reminding Lacey of all the things that had to be done around the house while they were gone. Now Lacey had resolved to seek adventure, and into her life had walked, or rolled, Jack.

He wasn't methodical. Or organized. He wasn't ever going to be either of those things, she suspected, smoothing the stacks of towels into the cabinet under the sink. But in the long run, how much did that matter? Surely not as much as the intensity or the passionate love for life, for her, and for his Lord that Jack Dalton brought with him. Butterflies needed nectar to live, not order and organization. That was for ants. And thanks to Jack, Lacey had sprouted wings. For once her praise to God was simple; all day she just kept whispering the same thing. "Thank you. Thank you."

Twenty-Three

Thursday afternoon Jack appeared on her doorstep, dressed in black jeans, a white shirt, and his usual shades and carrying a large square box wrapped in shimmering shiny paper. "Where do I put it? And don't change your mind, because it's heavy."

The light glinted off the shiny wrapping in a dull red sheen, and Lacey could hardly resist peeking at the tag or rattling the package. Jack wasn't letting her do either. "Put it on the dining-room table," she directed him, and he set it there with a deep, solid sound.

"Got time for a glass of tea and a chat?" she asked, smoothing out the cotton skirt she'd worn all day.

"Not now."

"How 'bout a quick hug, then?" Lacey walked over and pushed that one lock of hair out of his face, reveling in the crisp texture of it.

"With you, they're never quick hugs, Lacey," Jack said, fire glinting in his eyes. "I've got to go drop by the Dunwoodys, then check the copy for the brochure Leona finished this morning." He kissed her briefly and smiled. "I just wanted to drive you crazy for twenty-four hours with this. I think I've gotten you the perfect present. Tell Becca I'll bring the ice cream. And tell Britt that, yes, some of it will be vanilla. And tell Brian I intend to come by bright and early Sunday morning to take everybody to church with me, since we all missed last week. Bye."

"Bye," Lacey echoed, still holding on to the door frame and

watching him leave. The original grasshopper, springing in and out before she could nail him down. She went over to examine the package. It was tied with a white ribbon, shiny and smooth, and the card was white with a few words jotted in Jack's angular handwriting. Lacey groaned as she read it. "My love is like…"

Ugh. "My love is like a red, red rose." Browning. She nudged the box and felt the weight of it. Just heavy enough to contain an entire set of leather-bound poetry books from the rare book store on Park Avenue. Expensive and just like Jack. It was kind of like Britt, who usually gave Lacey candy—Britt's favorite kind. How was she going to handle this?

Lacey looked at the box again and wondered what she'd say tomorrow night when she opened it. Then she stopped in her tracks. "No, Lord, this isn't right. Jack just told me he thought he had gotten me the perfect present. He's trusting you to give him everything he needs again, and I am too. So in that box is the perfect present for me. Thank you." She walked away from the box, now content not to touch it.

When the doorbell rang the next evening, Lacey could hardly get her second earring fastened. "Somebody answer that," she called, listening to a set of large tennis shoes thud down the stairs. There was lots of conversation in the living room. Smoothing her new red shorts, she checked the mirror one last time. Everything looked pretty good, given the limited amount of sleep she had gotten. The soft white cotton shirt accented what color she had left to her complexion, and she didn't really look as if she had been bent over the keyboard of her computer and on the phone until half an hour ago when she showered and changed.

She passed inspection, if Jack's whistle was anything to go

by. "I had Britt put the ice cream in the freezer," he said. "Happy birthday." The wink he gave her was a better present than the one sitting on the table.

"Haven't opened it yet? I thought your curiosity would get to you," Jack said.

"I open no present before its time," Lacey said, pursing her lips. "Unlike some people, who probably have to rewrap everything under the Christmas tree."

"Sometimes I only pick at the corners," Jack said with a laugh. "But now, Lacey, it is time."

It wasn't going to wait any longer. Jack's eyes were glowing in anticipation, and the kids were all clustered around the box. Brian jostled Britt, and she jiggled the box with her elbow. It made a sound, a soft, heavy whirr.

Lacey had heard that sound before, but it had not come from leather-bound sets of Browning. *Whirr.* The heavy purr of...weighted ball bearings. Her heart started pounding as she ripped open the Mylar wrapping and pushed aside the ribbon. The box was taped securely shut, and she nearly ruined a nail destroying the tape.

When she threw open the lid, she couldn't resist a scream. The roller skates nestled inside the box were perfect.

"When I was a kid we would have called this fire-engine red," Jack said. "I figured you would rather have these in that color than that awful neon yellow most fire engines are painted now."

"You're right," Lacey said, flinging herself into his arms and nearly smothering him with a kiss. "You are so very right."

Britt hefted one of the skates out of the box. "They even have silver glitter laces, Aunt Lacey," she said in a hushed, awed voice. She spun one of the wheels, and that dull purr rolled into Lacey's ears again.

It was a purr that said more than words ever could. It said, "Go off and have fun, and I'll support all your efforts." It said, "I know who you are, and I like you that way." It was the voice of a warm, creative individual who liked butterflies. Behind that whirr was the laughter of heaven at this unlikely pair finally getting together.

Jack picked her up and gently swung her around once. "There's more outside."

"More?" Lacey couldn't resist a long laugh that ended on a rising note. "What more could there be?"

"Come and see," Jack said, leading her out the door by the hand.

In the driveway sat a large red four-by-four sport-utility vehicle. It had loud stripes and huge tires and gleamed like the grin on Jack's face. Lacey looked at it and burst into tears. "Yes," she said when she could get her breath back. "Yes. Yes. Yes. But, Jack, most people settle for an engagement band."

"Jewelry wouldn't mean the same thing coming from me. So I'm different," he said. "When?"

Brian, standing behind them, looked from one to the other, rubbing his head. "You said yes, but I didn't hear him ask you anything, Aunt Lacey."

"Sometimes, my friend, actions speak louder than words," Jack said.

Inside, the phone pealed shrilly. "Somebody get that," Lacey said, using the heel of her hand to wipe her cheek. The kids all raced for the phone, and Britt won.

"It's Brooke," she yelled, probably deafening her sister for life. She chattered away to her for a minute. "And then she said most people settle for an engagement band. Do you get it, Brooke?" She cocked her head, listening. "Oh," she said, dropping the receiver on the couch and racing for the front door.

"Aunt Lacey, Brooke wants to know if you can wait until Easter Sunday when her spring break starts. Do I get to be a flower girl?"

"I expect so," Lacey said dreamily. "Somebody go talk to Brooke."

"I still don't get it," Brian said, looking at his sister. Brittany put an arm around him.

"It's like this, Brian," she said, leading him inside. "Aunt Lacey and Uncle Jack are going to get married. You can even ask Brooke. She says so."

"Really?" he asked, looking behind him doubtfully at the two of them.

"Really," they chorused before Jack picked Lacey up and swung her around with a whoop.

"Easter, huh?" Jack said. "That's weeks. I'm not sure I can wait that long."

"Well, you'll have to. I don't think I could put things together any quicker than that anyway. I would like to meet your father before then…"

"Naturally. He'll love you."

Lacey made a face. "You love me, and that's what counts."

He kissed her softly, gently, with promise. "Thank you for saying that. And you're right. I do love you." Jack pushed open the screen door and deposited Lacey inside. "Go make plans with Brooke, and get her home as soon as possible."

Once Lacey hung up the phone, everyone started talking at once except Jack. He just sat on one end of the couch, smiling and watching his new family go crazy. Becca was insisting that the bridesmaids wear black. "As long as there are ruffles and lace, who cares what color it is? And then I could wear it again."

Brian was lobbying for a reception catered by the Greek

pizzeria. "I'll bet they'd do it. And think how much money you'd save."

Lacey opened her mouth to answer both of them, but Britt beat her to it. "I'm very, very hungry," she said loudly. "And thirsty. You need to help me get the ice cream and cake and iced tea ready for the party." With that, she took her brother and sister by the hand and started dragging them out of the room.

"What are you doing that for?" Brian asked.

Brittany was truly trying to whisper. But even her whisper would carry for half a block. "I want them to be alone. They're in love, silly. Besides, I'm tired of being the baby. I want cousins. And the more we leave them alone—"

"Oh, is that how it works?" Jack murmured, drawing Lacey into his arms.

"When you're seven, that's all there is to it," Lacey said.

He slid her glasses off and put them on the end table. "We might have to practice a while before we get the hang of it. I don't know how many cousins Britt wants."

"We could ask her," Lacey said with a wicked grin. As she drew a deep breath to do just that, Jack silenced her with a kiss.

"Knowing Britt, she's going to want at least a dozen," Jack said. "Do you think we can handle that?" He looked up as the children flicked off the light switch.

"Hey, we can handle anything, with the right kind of help. The kind we already have just for the asking," Lacey said, her voice choked with happy tears.

Jack ran a finger down the bridge of her nose. "We'd better get up. Here comes your birthday cake. You need to make a wish."

Lacey looked at the faces bathed in candlelight around her,

dwelling on each one before she came back to Jack, his eyes shining with love. "Nothing left to wish for, Jackson. God's already given me everything I could ever want."

"Given it to us both, Lacey," Jack whispered in the flickering light. "Personally I can't thank him enough. But that won't keep me from trying."

There in the warmth of love and light, Lacey felt her heart overflow. "That's true. We can always keep trying." When she blew out the candles, the gentle radiance still seemed to surround them all, shining like the joy in her heart.

Dear Reader,

Part of the idea for *Dalton's Dilemma* has been with me for a very long time, and came out of one of those situations that arises for all of us who have children, and some of us who don't.

Over a decade ago, when my husband's sisters were raising small children and teenagers, and we had two in the infant and preschool stage, we all faced that hard decision of who would raise our children if we were no longer alive. We all named each other as guardians, and my husband and I came to the realization that our family of two small boys could grow overnight into a family of six children, some of them already in high school.

None of that came to pass, and in fact our nieces and nephews are almost all adults with jobs, some with spouses, and in one lovely case a baby son (Hi, Bud) to liven up family gatherings. But the thought stayed with me: how does a family cope in a situation where parenthood is thrust upon someone not by the usual process of birth or adoption, but overnight? Finally in *Dalton's Dilemma* I got to explore that question.

Lacey's journey in fiction, along with my own in reality, has led me to the same conclusion. Our loving Father always has us in the palm of his hand, ready to lead us through any situation where we can relinquish control to him. I hope that your walk in Christ is filled with the peace that only he can give.

Sincerely,

Lynn Bulock

Write to Lynn Bulock
c/o Palisades
P.O. Box 1720
Sisters, Oregon 97759

THE PALISADES LINE

Look for these new releases at your local bookstore. If the title you seek is not in stock, the store may order you a copy using the ISBN listed.

Dalton's Dilemma, Lynn Bulock
ISBN 1-57673-238-X

Lacey Robbins, single mother of her sister's four children, is seeking adventure. But she never expected to find it by running into—literally!—handsome Jack Dalton at the roller rink. And she never expected the attraction between them to change her life forever....

Heartland Skies, Melody Carlson
ISBN 1-57673-264-9

Jayne Morgan moves to the small town of Paradise with the prospect of marriage, a new job, and plenty of horses to ride. But when her fiancé dumps her, she's left with loose ends. Then she wins a horse in a raffle, and the handsome rancher who boards her horse makes things look decidedly better.

Shades of Light, Melody Carlson (August 1998)
ISBN 1-57673-283-5

When widow Gwen Sullivan's daughter leaves for college, she discovers she can't bear her empty nest and takes a job at an interior decorating firm. But tedious work and a fussy boss leave her wondering if she's made the right move. Then Oliver Black, a prominent businessman, solicits her services and changes her mind....

Memories, Peggy Darty
ISBN 1-57673-171-5

In this sequel to *Promises,* Elizabeth Calloway is left with amnesia after witnessing a hit-and-run accident. Her husband, Michael, takes her on a vacation to Cancún so that she can relax and recover her memory. What they don't realize is that a killer is following them, hoping to wipe out Elizabeth's memory permanently....

Spirits, Peggy Darty (October 1998)
ISBN 1-57673-304-1

Picking up where *Memories* left off, the Calloways take a vacation to Angel Valley to find a missing woman. They enlist the help of a local writer who is an expert in Smoky Mountain legend, and uncover a strange web of folklore and spirits.

Remembering the Roses, Marion Duckworth
ISBN 1-57673-236-3

Sammie Sternberg is trying to escape her memories of the man who betrayed her and ends up in a small town on the Olympic Peninsula in Washington. There she opens her dream business—an antique shop in an old Victorian—and meets a reclusive watercolor artist who helps to heal her broken heart.

Waterfalls, Robin Jones Gunn
ISBN 1-57673-221-5

In a visit to Glenbrooke, Oregon, Meredith Graham meets movie star Jacob Wilde and is sure he's the one. But when Meri puts her foot in her mouth, things fall apart. Is isn't until the two of them get thrown together working on a book-and-movie project that Jacob realizes his true feelings, and this time he's the one who's starstruck.

China Doll, Barbara Jean Hicks
ISBN 1-57673-262-2

Bronson Bailey is having a mid-life crisis: after years of globe-trotting in his journalism career, he's feeling restless. Georgine Nichols has also reached a turning point: after years of longing for a child, she's decided to adopt. The problem is, now she's fallen in love with Bronson, and he doesn't want a child.

Angel in the Senate, Kristen Johnson Ingram
ISBN 1-57673-263-0

Newly elected senator Megan Likely heads to Washington with high hopes for making a difference in government. But accusations of election fraud, two shocking murders, and threats on her life make the Senate take a back seat. She needs to find answers, but she's not sure who she can trust anymore.

Irish Rogue, Annie Jones
ISBN 1-57673-189-8

Michael Shaughnessy has paid the price for stealing a pot of gold, and now he's ready to make amends to the people he's hurt. Fiona O'Dea is number one on his list. The problem is, Fiona doesn't want to let Michael near enough to hurt her again. But before she knows it, he's taken his Irish charm and worked his way back into her life…and her heart.

Beloved, Deb Kastner (August 1998)
ISBN 1-57673-331-9

Wanted: A part-time pastor with a full-time heart for a wedding ministry. When wedding coordinator Kate Logan places the ad for a pastor, she doesn't expect a man like Todd Jensen to apply. But she quickly learns that he's perfect for the job—and perfect for her heart.

On Assignment, Marilyn Kok
ISBN 1-57673-279-7
When photographer Tessa Brooks arrives in Singapore for an assignment, she's both excited and nervous about seeing her ex-fiancé, banker Michael Lawton. Michael has mixed feelings, too: he knows he still loves Tessa, but will he ever convince her that they can get past the obstacle of their careers and make their relationship work?

Forgotten, Lorena McCourtney
ISBN 1-57673-222-3
A woman wakes up in an Oregon hospital with no memory of who she is. When she's identified as Kat Cavanaugh, she returns to her home in California. As Kat struggles to recover her memory, she meets a fiancé she doesn't trust and an attractive neighbor who can't believe how she's changed. She begins to wonder if she's really Kat Cavanaugh, but if she isn't, what happened to the real Kat?

Canyon, Lorena McCourtney (September 1998)
ISBN 1-57673-287-8
Kit Holloway and Tyler McCord are wildly in love, planning their wedding, and looking forward to a summer of white-water rafting through the Grand Canyon. Then the actions of two people they love rip apart their relationship. Can their love survive, or will their differences prove to be too much?

Rustlers, Karen Rispin (September 1998)
ISBN 1-57673-292-4
Amber Lacey is on the run—from her home, from her career, and from God. She ends up working on a ranch in western

Alberta and trying to keep the secrets of her past from the man she's falling in love with. But then sinister dealings on the ranch force Amber to confront the mistakes she's made—and turn back to the God who never gave up on her.

The Key, Gayle Roper
ISBN 1-57673-223-1
On Kristie Matthews's first day living on an Amish farm, she gets bitten by a dog and is rushed to the emergency room by a handsome stranger. In the ER, an elderly man in the throes of a heart attack hands her a key and tells her to keep it safe. Suddenly odd accidents begin to happen to her, but no one's giving her any answers.

The Document, Gayle Roper (October 1998)
ISBN 1-57673-295-9
While Cara Bentley is sorting through things after the death of her grandfather, she stumbles upon evidence that he was adopted. Determined to find her roots, she heads to Lancaster County and settles in at an Amish farm. She wants to find out who she is, but she can't help wondering: if it weren't for the money in John Bentley's will, would anyone else care about her identity?

ANTHOLOGIES

Fools for Love, Ball, Brooks, Jones
ISBN 1-57673-235-5
By Karen Ball: Kitty starts pet-sitting, but when her clients turn out to be more than she can handle, she enlists help from a handsome handyman.

By Jennifer Brooks: Caleb Murphy tries to acquire a book collection from a widow, but she has one condition: he must marry her granddaughter first.

By Annie Jones: A college professor who has been burned by love vows not to be fooled twice, until her ex-fiancé shows up and ruins her plans!

Heart's Delight, Ball, Hicks, Noble
ISBN 1-57673-220-7

By Karen Ball: Corie receives a Valentine's Day date from her sisters and thinks she's finally found the one...until she learns she went out with the wrong man.

By Barbara Jean Hicks: Carina and Reid are determined to break up their parents' romance, but when it looks like things are working, they have a change of heart.

By Diane Noble: Two elderly bird-watchers set aside their differences to try to save a park from disaster, but learn they've bitten off more than they can chew.

Be sure to look for any of the 1997 titles you may have missed:

Surrender, Lynn Bulock (ISBN 1-57673-104-9)
Single mom Cassie Neel accepts a blind date from her children for her birthday.

Wise Man's House, Melody Carlson (ISBN 1-57673-070-0)
A young widow buys her childhood dream house, and a mysterious stranger moves into her caretaker's cottage.

Moonglow, **Peggy Darty** (ISBN 1-57673-112-X)
Tracy Kosell comes back to Moonglow, Georgia, and investigates a case with a former schoolmate, who's now a detective.

Promises, **Peggy Darty** (ISBN 1-57673-149-9)
A Christian psychologist asks her detective husband to help her find a dangerous woman.

Texas Tender, **Sharon Gillenwater** (ISBN 1-57673-111-1)
Shelby Nolan inherits a watermelon farm and asks the sheriff for help when two elderly men begin digging holes in her fields.

Clouds, **Robin Jones Gunn** (ISBN 1-57673-113-8)
Flight attendant Shelly Graham runs into her old boyfriend, Jonathan Renfield, and learns he's engaged.

Sunsets, **Robin Jones Gunn** (ISBN 1-57673-103-0)
Alissa Benson has a run-in at work with Brad Phillips, and is more than a little upset when she finds out he's her neighbor!

Snow Swan, **Barbara Jean Hicks** (ISBN 1-57673-107-3)
Toni, an unwed mother and a recovering alcoholic, falls in love for the first time. But if Clark finds out the truth about her past, will he still love her?

Irish Eyes, **Annie Jones** (ISBN 1-57673-108-1)
Julia Reed gets drawn into a crime involving a pot of gold and has her life turned upside-down by Interpol agent Cameron O'Dea.

Father by Faith, **Annie Jones** (ISBN 1-57673-117-0)
Nina Jackson buys a dude ranch and hires cowboy Clint Cooper as her foreman, but her son, Alex, thinks Clint is his new daddy!

Stardust, **Shari MacDonald** (ISBN 1-57673-109-X)
Gillian Spencer gets her dream assignment but is shocked to learn she must work with Maxwell Bishop, who once broke her heart.

Kingdom Come, **Amanda MacLean** (ISBN 1-57673-120-0)
Ivy Rose Clayborne, M.D., pairs up with the grandson of the coal baron to fight the mining company that is ravaging her town.

Dear Silver, **Lorena McCourtney** (ISBN 1-57673-110-3)
When Silver Sinclair receives a letter from Chris Bentley ending their relationship, she's shocked, since she's never met the man!

Enough! **Gayle Roper** (ISBN 1-57673-185-5)
When Molly Gregory gets fed up with her three teenaged children, she announces that she's going on strike.

A Mother's Love, **Bergren, Colson, MacLean** (ISBN 1-57673-106-5)
Three heartwarming stories share the joy of a mother's love.

Silver Bells, **Bergren, Krause, MacDonald** (ISBN 1-57673-119-7)
Three novellas focus on romance during Christmastime.